A HIGHER CALLING

A Higher Calling

David C. Weekley

Inquiries: dcweekley@ualr.edu

Contents

Dedication	vi
Chapter 1	1
Chapter 2	16
Chapter 3	24
Chapter 4	29
Chapter 5	38
Chapter 6	49
Chapter 7	61
Chapter 8	76
Chapter 9	86
Chapter 10	105
Chapter 11	110
Chapter 12	115
About The Author	122

Dedicated in memory of my friend,
Steve Pausche.

Thanks to Amanda Hathcock for
story clarification
and Cindi Rudes for being my editor.

Copyright © 2021 by David C. Weekley

All rights reserved. No part of this book may be reproduced in any manner whatsoever without written permission except in the case of brief quotations embodied in critical articles and reviews.

3rd edition

First Printing, 2021

Chapter 1

Harpoon Barry's Tattoos

Shadow, a tall and lanky dude with colored tattoos on each arm, leaned up against the brick wall of the dingy shop with a twirly, swirly brightly colored sign on the window that said, "Harpoon Barry's Tattoos". The buildings in this part of town dated back to the early 1900s; many of which were abandoned and in disrepair. However, with a little work the owner, Barry, was able to make his shop a very cheap place of business close to a bustling downtown of Galveston, Texas. Barry was lanky with an unkempt goatee and a wooden pirate-like peg leg. He had lost his leg in a car accident and decided the peg leg would work perfect for his business, hence, the founding of the name "Harpoon Barry's Tattoos". Galveston island was a major port on the coast of Texas founded by pirates in the early 1800s. So Barry's business fit right in with the culture. His business made a great location for the shadowy business of the local drug dealer, Shadow. He would give Barry some reefer (marijuana) in return for use of the premises.

A psychedelic Volkswagen, typical for a hippie in the early 1970s, screeched around the corner and stopped abruptly in front of the shop. Everyone knew it was Dave Brinkley's VW because there was no other like it. Dave painted it with model car paints. He would make a paisley shape with one color and then another swirly shape with another color, sort of like the way jig saw puzzle pieces fit together, only more psychedelic. He painted a black border around the shapes to help them stand out. The model car paints were about 15 cents apiece at that time yet the quality was amazingly professional. However, the metal flake colors faded over time.

Dave got out of the bug with his sidekick, Jake Evans. From the side his billowy afro obscured his face. You could only see his face if you looked at him head on. He wore his favorite tie-dye t-shirt and bell bottomed jeans that covered his feet. The edges were frayed from walking on them. Jake adorned himself with a tank top, shorts, and sandals. His long curly, bushy hair hung down to his shoulder blades. He looked around, paranoid, and pushed up his round wire rim glasses.

As they approached Shadow, Dave scratched his butt saying "What ya got today?"

Shadow reached into the side pocket of his leather vest. "Hey, man... Got some Purple Haze." Purple Haze was a tiny purple tablet of LSD (lysergic acid diethylamide); a mind altering, psychedelic drug that produced hallucinations and euphoria.

Jake looked Shadow straight in the eye. "How much?"

` "Three bucks a hit."

With wrinkled brow and slightly raised voice Dave said, "What?". He paused a second. "I heard it was two bucks!"

Shadow shook his head and grinned like he had a little secret. "That's for quantity, man. Supply and demand. Now, the supply is low and the demand is high." Jake looking at

Dave over his wire rim glasses shook his head. Nervously he stutters, "Ca..ca..can we do th..th..this inside, please?"

Shadow made a grandeur, sweeping gesture toward the door. They entered the dimly lit tattoo parlor. A high pitched vibrating sound filled the room. Adorning the walls were Barry's original artwork with psychedelic patterns and mythical creatures, a stop sign and a couple of street signs. A huge, burly shrimper dude was sitting next to a dusty work bench, arrayed with various tattoos. Barry nodded at the three walking in as he worked away on the man's tattoo.

With a tattoo iron in one hand and a smoldering joint in the other he busily worked on the man's back. (A joint is a hand rolled marijuana cigarette. When smoked it would produce euphoria, altered states of mental activity and sense of time, and difficulty with concentration and memory.) He took a huge toke on the blunt, and handed it to Shadow as he choked the smoke down holding back a cough. Shadow took a huge, long hit on the joint and handed it to Dave.

Dave said as he took the joint. "So... what's up?"

Barry coughs out a blast of smoke. "I'm wasted, man."

Dave sucked some smoke in and passed the smoldering joint on to Jake. Looking at the tattoo on the Shrimper's back he quietly read, "I'm a doper, I'm a smoker, I'm a shimp boat rider: and if you don't like it fuc..." Dave laughs out loud releasing the smoke from his lungs. He didn't have the heart to tell Barry that he misspelled shrimp.

Barry frowned. "Don't waste that stuff. It's Panama Red."

Dave grinning from ear to ear said, "Sorry, got carried away."

Jake drew a long toke and speaks while holding it in. "So... let... let's get to business."

Jake handed Barry back his joint as Barry pointed to the back room saying, "Make yourselves at home. Mi casa es su casa!"

Shadow opened the creaky door to the dusty back room. The stuff stacked up in the room would have felt at place in a flea market. With no place to sit they piled in the room standing close together. Jake leaned against a table stacked with junk and knocked a vase off but caught it before it hit the ground.

"Whoa, that was close!" Shadow said amazed at the catch.

Dave started chuckling again thinking about the shrimper's tattoo.

"What on earth are you laughing about? That wasn't that funny and I know you're not that fucked up," Shadow said.

Dave said shaking his head, "Did you see the tattoo Larry was working on? What a hoot."

Scratching his head Jake said, "Didn't notice."

Dave chuckled shaking his head. "It said, ' I'm a doper, I'm a smoker, I'm a shimp boat rider.' Larry misspelled shrimp."

Shadow laughed. "Whose going to break the news to that monster of a guy?"

They all laughed.

Dave said, "No one. After that the tat says 'if you don't like it fuck you'." They all joined in with some gut busting laughter.

Jake said, "Crazy dude... How'd he get the peg leg?"

Dave responded, "In a car crash. They had to amputate. He decided a peg leg would be good for his business. He wrote it off his income tax as advertising." Shadow piped in, "He files income tax?... I don't think he has a leg to stand on." The others chuckled.

Shadow ready to get to business said, " How much of this stuff you guys want?"

Jake pulling out his wallet took a peek inside. "For the right price I'll take 5 hits."

"Give me ten. That deserves a discount." Dave grabbed his wallet. "How much?"

Shadow pulled out a baggy of tiny purple tablets from his back pack grinning broadly, "Not enough for a disount. Like I said, 3 bucks."

Dave shook his head and pulled out some bills from his wallet. "OK... OK... Got any of that Panama Red?"

Panama Red was a higher quality type of marjuana that grew in Panama. It's high was dumbfounding. Dave often called a joint a "procrastin stick" because when high he would procrastinate and not get much done. For example, it took him eight years to get an Associates Degree at a community college. After that he sort of gave up on getting his Bachelor's Degree at a University. Too busy getting high.

Farming Country

Officer Ward and his partner, Jimbo, stood in a circle with a farmer in a corn field about twenty yards off the dirt road. Officer Ward was a man in his forties with streaks of gray hair and a protruding "beer" belly. Jimbo was a skinny dude who refused to wear his police hat and preferred a ball cap with a Colt gun company logo. The corn was just a few inches tall. Their interest wasn't corn but the young plant with pointy leaves. Yes, someone had planted a marijuana plant in the farmer's field. Officer Ward was puffing on a cigar as the farmer explained the situation.

The cops back then were mostly known as redneck. There was a literal application and a figurative application to that term. The literal was that they mostly had their haircut above the ears leaving the back of their neck exposed. Hence, when out in the sun it would get sunburned making it red. But, on the figurative note it meant they were very "country bumpkin" and hated the youth running around with long hair doing drugs. They called the hippies "girls", "Commie fags" (implying they were communists), "queer" and a sundry other derogatory terms. Then, they would chuckle like the term was a big joke. Many of them rode in pick up trucks with a rifle rack on the back window. Now, Dave with his huge afro drew a lot of attention from these folks. One sheep rancher came into a breakfast restaurant where Dave sat eating and put his hand on Dave's shoulder and said, "I wish my sheep had hair like you, son. What did ya do? Stick your finger in a light socket." Then, he laughed out loud as though he just made it up. However, Dave had heard the light socket one before. But, the rancher was nice about it. Most who voiced their disapproval were quite rude and showed their obvious anger.

So, they stood looking down at Dave's little plant in the corn field. The farmer pointed toward the dirt road and said, "I was driving down this here road and saw this damn long haired hippie with a shovel. So, I just drove on by acting like I didn't notice..." He spit some chewing tobacco on the ground. "I came back later and this is what I found."

Office Ward kneeled down to get a closer look. "Yep, it's marijuana, alright." He stood up looking intently at the farmer. "What's this dirt bag look like?"

"He had this huge ball of hair. An afro... Thought he was a nigger at first... scrawny dude... drove a psychedelic Volkswagen."

Officer ward nodded his head and rubbed his chin. "Uh huh. We know that S-O-B." He flicked the ash off his cigar like it was an exclamation point. "Would love to get my hands on him... 'Specially for cultivation. That's a felony."

Jimbo added, "Yep." He chuckled a goofy, Gomer Pyle, laugh. "We can send 'em up for a long time for this."

Purple Haze

Dave and Jake sat in Dave's psychedelic VW (Volkswagen) by the boardwalk on Seawall Boulevard. The seawall was a wall built after the 1900 hurricane to hold back high water. The 1900 storm wiped out Galveston. The seawall was 17 feet high and 10 miles long. Engineers worked to lift much of the city up to match the height of the wall. Some larger buildings lost their first floor. The seawall was a concrete wall that curved inward next to the beach with a wide sidewalk on top and benches for people to sit. There were stairs built into the wall for those wanting to spend time on the beach. The Seawall Boulevard was four lanes of traffic that paralleled the beach and went for the length of the city. So they sat in dumbfounded splendor playing music on an 8 track player. 8 track tape players were new tech at that time and did not fit well in the V-dub (slang for Volkswagen). So, it went in the glove box with wires hanging out for power and the ten inch speaker in the back seat; the lid of the glove box provided support to the bulky tape deck. "Purple Haze", a song by Jimi Hedrix, blasted from the speaker. Purple Haze, as stated before, was LSD that came in tiny purple tabs. The music was appropriate for their state of mind.

Jake stared blankly out of the window. "Crap, I'm wasted. Hope you can drive."

Dave very slowly turns his head to look at Jake. "Huh?"

"Looks like everything's breathing."

Dave mumbled with some slurring, "Yea, man... Like an ocean, man." "You're crazy. How can you do two hits. I can barely handle one."

The purple haze was kicking in and the ground rolled like ocean swells deep at sea. The sounds of traffic, people walking and talking, and hammers banging from a distant construction site all blended in together to make a harmonic rhythm that blended in with Jimi Hendrix's heavy lead guitar. It was a surreal transformation of the senses world that surpassed the psychedelic world of Alice in Wonderland. The cars streaming by had "trails" where the moving object would leave fading transparent visual echoes as they traveled by. The sky and clouds were swirling with color like multiple and varied drops of food color in a jar of water.

Dave grabbed the door handle and cracked open the creaky car door. "I've got to get up and moving. I think this stuff is cut with some speed."

"Na..na..not so sure 'bout that. I'm pa..pa..paranoid."

Dave stumbled out of the car flinging his door open and an oncoming car swerved and blew his horn as it almost unhinged the wide-open door.

"Wa..wa..watch out!", Jake cried. "There's cars out there!"

"No, shit, man."

Dave staggered over the curb and sat on the psychedelic hood. Jake dizzily caught his balance as he got out of the car. The ground moved in great swells causing him to stumble and sway as he walked.

Dave laughed out loud. "The ground is moving!!! Heavy stuff!!!"

Jake laughing, "Yeah, this is wild. The traffic sounds like drums... getting some great patterns and trails off the cars."

They strolled down the street with each step like stepping into a hole. Two Jesus freaks approached them with tracks in hand. Tracks were pamphlets from their ministry usually on how to get saved. They were dressed in slacks and nice shirts with short hair trimmed above the ear. One of them boldly struts up with child-like enthusiasm as the other timidly follows. "Excuse me", he said, "I'm here to tell you that Jesus loves you. And, you must.... blah, blah…". The Jesus freak's words were garbled in the minds of our two hippies and blended in with the traffic sounds which produced tribal beats to the tune of the sea breeze that seemed to swirl around the atmosphere with a variety of rainbow colors. Was this a run on sentence or could they decipher the message.

Dave played along. "Really...? Wow!"

Our Jesus freak gestured with his hand enthusiastically as Dave heard some phrases from the jumble of syllables, "… blah, blah… must confess all your sins…"

Dave nodded his head in acknowledgement. "Wow, this is great news!" "…blah… blah… repent and be baptized…"

"Tell me more."

"Garble, garble…it's a higher calling!"

"A higher calling? That's what I want!" he yelled. Then, he said calmly as he got closer to the religious dude's face looking him in the eye. "You got any LSD? That's the high that's calling me." Dave and Jake laughed. "See ya, buddy."

Dave and Jake walked away leaving the Jesus freak with his mouth wide open; flabbergasted.

Jake chuckled. "Man, the look on his face was priceless. You blew him out of the water."

"Jesus freaks just get under my skin. If they really had something to say, it would be one thing. Just a shallow sales pitch doesn't cut it with me. Jesus loves you… Jesus loves you." He said sarcastically. "Just a broken record… so shallow!"

A couple of police cars were up ahead parked next to the seawall boardwalk with lights flashing.

Jake shook his head, "Tha..that don't look good. I know we gotta look ha..ha..high as a kite."

"Yep, I think it's time to blow this pop stand."

Dave and Jake did an about face and headed in the opposite direction.

The Third Eye

Mary, a slender young lady in a flowing silky mini-skirt pranced right up to Shadow who leaned against the brick of the tattoo shop.

Shadow tipped his invisible hat. "Hey, sweetie. Come to brighten up my day?" He opened his arms wide for a hug but Mary pulled away.

"You know why I'm here... and it's not for you!"

"Aw... come on... Got some good Purple Haze."

"Last trip with Dave freaked me out." she said reaching into her bag for her wallet. "A bag will do just fine." Mary was referring to a psilocybin mushroom trip that she did with Dave. Psilocybin was a psychedelic drug similar to LSD or mescaline. The effects included euphoria, hallucinations, distortions in time and perception and a general sense of oneness with the surroundings. The cattle fields close to where Dave lived were full of these kinds of mushrooms; consequently Dave would frequent them often searching the cow shit where they grew. "So...sure seems like Dave is taking a liking to you. Huh?"

"It's really none of your business..." Mary furled her face up a bit, "but, I'm sick of it... He's been drinking a lot of mushroom tea lately. He's really strange on that stuff..."

"How so?"

"Says it opens up spiritual channels. Something about the third eye and some cosmic mumbo jumbo."

Shadow leaned his chin on his hand in deep thought. "The third eye. I heard something about that in an Eastern religions class. You meditate on a point in the middle of the forehead. Supposed to bring enlightenment."

"Can't really picture you sitting in a class."

"Don't know why I took that stupid class except that I needed the hours and it fit my schedule... Besides... had to quit that college shit. I'm doing better selling drugs than a silly diploma will do for me. But...don't worry about Dave. Don't think he would hurt a fly."

"I know. He was brought up in a good Christian home."

"Jeez, Mary. Don't get religious on me."

"Well... whatever... he's loosing it. Whenever he's straight he's depressed. The only time he's not depressed is when he's high. It's getting me down. So, I just... just need to break it off."

"His loss. I'm still available."

"Good for you... Got a bag?"

"Got some Panama Red."

Looking around to see if anyone was looking Mary and Shadow slipped stealthily into the shop.

Party Hardy

Jake and Dave shared rent on a small two bed room house in a small community close to the fisherman's wharf. At $110 a month it was very affordable for a couple of hippies that spent most of their money on drugs. They didn't even have to pay for utilities. It was a bit under-furnished with a worn couch in the center. The coffee table was a four foot long 2x12 board sitting on two old milk crates. The lamp was on a milk crate at one end of the couch. A huge, candle-wax mountain sat on the center of the coffee table. They would burn candles at night while getting high, the more different colors the better. In fact, they would randomly melt crayons from the flame of the candle to add a bit of flare. By changing the location of the candles each time it had peaks and valleys just like a mountain would. It was an ongoing, ever-changing work of art.

Still high on Purple Haze, Dave and Jake relaxed on the couch. The music was blasting loudly as they sat on the sofa sharing a fat 4 inch joint made by using several rolling papers. It was really an acquired skill to roll one of those monsters. Jake coughs up a huge blast of smoke. "This is some good shit. It's really smoothing out the rough edges of this acid." Acid was slang for LSD. It was usually cut with speed and strychnine which made it come on heavier however that contributed to nervous jitters as it came on and achy joints and muscles when coming down. Marijuana helped the jitters and achy joints.

Dave responded with 3 big nods of the head. "No shit, man. I'm getting some great colors and patterns... I was just thinking about that... that..." He paused with that deer in the headlights glazed stare. "Can't remember what I was going to say."

"Can't help ya there!"

They laughed and continued passing the joint with a short cough after almost every hit. Dave turned to lean against the arm of the couch. "You know peyote cactus is legal for Indians because it's part of their religion." The psychedelic drug mescaline was produced from the peyote cactus.

"I can dig that kind of religion!"

They paused staring off into nothing. Dave said, "I'm flabbergasted plastered!" He closed his eyes. "Hey, I close my eyes and I see a pulsating purple blob. I think it's my aura."

"You're aura?"

"Everyone has an aura, man... got to get into third eye consciousness to see it."

Jake scratched his head. "You... you've been reading too much!" "Reading's good. It helps me write."

"Well... I've got a better explanation for your aura."

"What?"

"You're sta... stoned out of your gourd."

They both laughed as Dave put the roach into the ashtray. It was called a roach when it was too small to handle. However, a roach clip (usually an alligator clip or locking medical forceps) was used at times to burn it all the way to the end. "Either way, that aura stuff is pretty cool..." Dave looked around the room. "Hey! Let's see if we can pull color out of the wall!"

Dave jumped out of his seat and ran over to the wall with Jake following. Dave leaned on his shoulder against the wall with his face close to the wall looking down it. With his finger twirling out from the wall he spun a green florescent glowing fiber optic-like thread that followed his finger forming a conical spiral. Jake follows suit with a red one. They continued to hypnotically spin various colors out of the wall for quite some time.

Later that evening Dave sits in the moonlight on the steps of the porch smoking a joint. He was feeling pretty rough as he crashed from his LSD trip. Whispering and looking down at the steps he said, "Well, God, here I am. Wasn't a bad day. Thanks for the fun times..." Taking a long draw on the joint and holding it in as long as possible he held in a cough and blew out the remainder of the smoke.

"I guess, I was a little hard on that Jesus freak. Sorry 'bout that. But, it really doesn't seem like they really know you, God. Not saying I'm any better but at least I don't act like I know. All's they say is Jesus loves you." He continued in a mocking tone, "'Jesus loves you… Jesus loves you.' Makes me sick. They don't tell you nothin'…" Shaking his head he said soberly, "Anyway… forgive me if I was hard on that guy… in the name of Jesus Christ." Dave always talked to God, not Jesus. He saw God as The Father and Jesus was His son. He knew it was because of what Jesus had accomplished that he had access to God. He was taught to always pray in the name of Jesus Christ if you wanted your prayers answered. So, he had a respect for God but was pretty critical of hell fire and brimstone preachers. His God was a God of love. Didn't know much more than that but, what he did know, he hung onto dearly.

Chapter 2

Trouble with the Law

Speeding down the dusty dirt farm road Dave looked for the spot in the corn fields where he planted his marijuana. Pulling up to a spot where a fox skin was hanging on the barbed wire fence he grabbed a small hoe and a bag of Marijuana seeds. Getting out of the car he struts up to the fence and carefully crawls between a couple of strands of barbed wire. When he gets to the planting spot he found his marijuana plant missing and a boot print in the soft dirt.

"Oh, crap!!!", he said.

He scrambled back to the car and drove off. At the same time a patrol car traveled down the same road with Officer Ward and Jimbo, his deputy.

Officer Ward said, "Heard they had a pretty good bust last night. Got a couple of bags and some LSD."

Jimbo rolled down the window to spit out some chewing tobacco. "Yea, but we still got a lot of hippie bastards to get. Damn degenerates. Ruining the country." They noticed a cloud of dust flying from a car ahead. As the dust cleared some Dave's psychedelic Volkswagen became visible.

Office Ward hung his head out the window for a better look. "Looks like Brinkley's Volkswagen up ahead." He put the pedal to the metal in hot pursuit. Dave looked in his rear view mirror and saw them coming. Speeding up he approached the main road and rolled his window down and grabbed his hoe and bag of seeds. Wheeling around the corner he threw them out into the ditch hoping they wouldn't see. The police car wheeled around the corner after him with lights flashing and siren blaring. Dave slowed down and pulled over with the police car behind. As the officers sauntered over Dave made his way to the back of the car. Dave said with all the naivety he could muster, "What's the problem?" Officer ward said gruffly, "You know damn well what the problem is. You've been growing that marija-wanna out in the fields and we just caught you red handed."

"Don't know what you're talking about ... sir", Dave said sarcastically.

"Just turn around and put your hands on the car... Frisk 'em Jimbo." Dave turned around and slapped his hands on the car as Jimbo proceeded to frisk him. Dave innocently said, "Now, why ya pulling me over. I wasn't speeding." Jimbo replied with noticeable aggitation, "We don't need a reason to pull you over, dirt bag!" Jimbo grabbed his privates.

Dave said cynically, "I know why you pulled me over. You needed someone to fondle."

The officer responded in his typical redneck way, "Why don't you just shut up, you punk! You queer ass mother fucker with your pussy-ass long hair. You make me sick." He winked at Dave and said, "I bet we can find something very interesting in that stupid looking car of yours."

Jimbo worked his way down Dave's legs. "Nothing on his body."

Officer Ward moved on to search the car while Jimbo guarded Dave. Officer Ward opened the glove box and pulled the 8 track player out ripping the wires out and throws it on the ground. He picked up one of the 8 track tapes. "Hmmm... Looks like a great place to hide some drugs." He breaks the tape case open and pulls out a spaghetti of tape. "Nope... nothing here." He proceeded to hurl car mats and anything loose from the car. Officer Ward popped out of the car holding a marijuana seed between his thumb and finger. "We got you... you son of a bitch! We're taking ya in!"

Jimbo put the cuffs on Dave.

Officer Ward smirked as he walked over to Dave. "We are charging you with cultivation of marijuana. And, that's a felony, boy. You're in deep doo doo, now!"

They both laughed mockingly, clearly enjoying the moment.

That evening Dave sat on a hard bench in the holding cell. Officer Ward walked into the cell puffing on a cigar. After blowing smoke from his cigar into Dave's face he said, "OK. We need to talk." He put his face a few inches from Dave's face.

Dave turned his head away from Officer Ward's penetrating look.

"Where you living now, boy? Your driver's license says you're livin' with your parents... I know better than that. Where ya livin'?"

Dave just turned to the wall.

Officer Ward grabbed him by his shirt and pulled him upright sticking his face in his face. "Answer me! You son of a bitch!" Then, he flung him against the wall. Dave fell in a heap groaning.

After kicking him hard in the side Officer Ward said, "Get

up you bastard and talk to me." Then, he laid another hard kick. "I said get up!"

Dave slowly got up and sat on the bench holding his side.

"OK. Let me put it to you this way. Since that's where you're supposed to be living we're going to search your parents' home. And, we're going to tear that place apart."

Dave, still grimacing from the blows said, "Leave my folks out of this. That ain't right."

"Don't you tell me what's fuckin' right. If you got anything stashed away at their house you better tell me."

"Fuck you!!!"

"If we find anything we're taking your parents to jail. After all it is their home..." After a deafening silence he said, "OK, if that's the way you want it." Officer Ward walked away, opened the door, and as he stepped halfway out Dave said, "Wait."

Officer Ward stopped mid-step and turned around. "OK. I'm listening."

"In my bedroom there's a bag in my suit coat."

Later that night Dave sat on a cell bunk alone. A drunk rambled on incoherently at the far end of the hall.

With his head bowed Dave whispers, "OK, God. Here I am in a mess again. I can't believe this shit keeps happening to me. I can't do anything right. Every step I take, I step in it. Well, anyway, you know all that. I'm asking... I'm begging, get me out of this mess... I'll do better. I promise. Thanks... in the name of Jesus Christ."

Dave punched up his hard mattress and laid himself back on his bunk. He rolled over on his side and stared blankly at the wall. "Wish I had a joint."

Trouble at Home

The next day at Dave's parents' house his mom busied herself with her normal chores and heard the door bell ring. When she opened the door she was surprised to see Officer Ward and Jimbo standing there.

Officer Ward very politely said, "Maam... we've got your son at our jail on a marijuana charge."

She puts her hand to her mouth in shock. "Oh, my..."

"He told us that he stashed a bag of pot in his suit pocket. Now, you can cooperate or we can take you and your husband to jail since it's in your house." She opened the door to let them in. "Oh, my... of course... whatever you need." Tears started rolling down her checks.

"Where's his room?"

Sobbing she said, "Down the hall to the left."

As the cops walked down the hall Dave's dad walked into the room. "What's going on?"

Dave's mom turned, fell into dad's arms, and sobbed on his shoulder.

The cops found the stash and as they left told the parents that they better get a lawyer.

That evening Mr. Fredericks, a lawyer and friend of the family, sat with Dave's folks at the kitchen table. Dave's mom had a handkerchief in her hand from crying.

Mr. Fredericks said, "Well, George... Bettye... when I was his scout master I never imagined I would have to defend him for this kind of thing. I can't believe it... And, he was only one merit badge from Eagle Scout."

George nodded, "He gave up on Scouts when he started doing drugs."

Bettye said, "Thank you so much for helping us. We can pay you for your time."

"Nope. Don't want it. That boy really means a lot to me. Just want to help."

George forced a smile. "Thank you so much. What's next?"

"Well... they found a seed in his car. You can't extract any THC out of a seed so there's really no evidence. They had no grounds to bust him to begin with. They had no search warrant when they came here. I should be able to get the judge to throw it out of court."

Bettye said with a sigh of relief, "Thank God."

Back to Work

An array of culvert forms were scattered across the construction yard and a concrete truck rolled up ready to pour. A culvert was a concrete structure built to drain water off a road. An office trailer had a sign over the door that said "J. R. Nettle Construction Co." Pete worked with Dave exclusively and they built concrete forms for bridges and culverts. Pete's brother-in-law, Clyde, was the job foreman. Clyde was short, broad shouldered and muscular with a full mountain-man beard. Pete and Dave smoked pot as they worked. Clyde didn't smoke that shit but allowed them to as long as they could put out the work. Pete and Dave were his best workers.

The base of culvert drains for the city roads were built

on site at the construction yard. They used to build them in ground on location but crawling in a hole or pumping water out after a rain seemed a bit cumbersome for Pete and Dave. So they started thinking about better ways to produce the culverts. If they built them all in one location they could crank them out. They could load them on a flat bed truck with a crane and drop them in the holes at each location. Of course,

Clyde loved the idea and that became the standard operation. Clyde was with Pete while he was tying steel on one of the concrete forms.

"Where the hell is Dave this morning", Clyde grumbled.

"Don't know." Pete said. "Maybe he had a late night."

"Yeah, probably smoking that shit all night."

They turned at the sound of squealing tires. Dave swerved to miss a car as he raced into the construction yard. A cloud of dust followed as he slammed on his breaks. Getting out of his car he shot his fist at the passing car yelling, "You could of hit me, you ass hole!" He grabbed his tool bag out of the car and strapped it around his waist walking briskly up to Clyde and Pete. "You see that. He almost smacked my rear end."

Clyde said with a disgruntled look, "All I saw was you driving like a bat out of hell. It's fuckin' 10:30. You partying half the night?"

"I got thrown in the slammer. Got busted for a seed. Can you believe that shit. A fuckin' seed."

Clyde said yelling, "We got concrete waiting. Get that steel tied now!!!" He threw his hands up in the air and shaking his head walked away.

Pete shaking his head said, "How many jobs are there

where you can smoke dope while you work? Better cool it if you want to keep this job." Pete pulled out a joint from his tool pouch, lit it up and took a long draw. Dave grabbed a few strands of tie wire and started tying some steel.

"Well, Clyde don't care. We're the best workers he's got." Dave said tying steel like a maniac.

Pete held in his cough and handed the joint to Dave.

Chapter 3

Trouble with Mary

Mary stood on the porch talking to Jake at their house. Dave pulled up from work and walked up to the porch.

Jake gave Mary a hug and walked out toward his car. In passing he patted Dave on the back saying, "Gotta get to work. Good luck!"

Dave looked at him quizzically as he walked up to Mary.

"Hey, Mary, good of ya to come over." Dave said as he moved toward her for a hug.

Mary pushed back looking obviously angry. "Hey, Dave."

"What's up love. You look pissed."

"Did you get busted last night?"

"Yeah, they caught me on the road where my plant was growing...", Dave said as he rubbed his eyes. "Are you upset about that? I was just at the wrong place at the wrong time."

"Look, it's like you've got a target on your back with that damn psychedelic bug. If I was with you, I'd of been busted, too."

"Look, honey. I'll be careful."

"Don't honey me! I ain't your honey." She threw up her hands in disgust. "I just can't do this anymore. I came here to break it off."

"Come on, let's talk. I got some good reefer. It'll calm you down."

"No! Damn it. It's just not working. I'm sorry. I care about ya. But, but I can't do this."

"C'mon, babe!"

"Don't call me babe! It's over... Damn you!" Mary walked briskly and defiantly away.

Dave stood motionless for a moment then turned to go indoors. Once inside he hits the wall with his fist. "I'm tired of this shit!" In a rage he kicked the coffee table across the room; the ashtray and bong went flying. He ripped his posters off the wall. Then, he slammed a chair against the wall putting a hole in the wall. He walked over to the stove and slammed his fist on the burner and broke the burner. Grabbing his hand he doubled over in pain. "Crap! Now, you've screwed up your hand. You stupid idiot!!!" He kicked a chair across the room.

Magic Mushrooms

Dave pulled up in his psychedelic bug next to a field sheltered on each side by trees. That he would do anything illicit in that car was like a billboard advertising "I'm here, cops, come and get me". Cows grazed in the field as he got out of the car with a plastic grocery bag in hand. He climbed through the barbed wire fence snagging and ripping the hem of his bell bottomed pants.

"Dang. I'm screwing everything up."

He moved among the grasses of the field searching for some shit. Psilocybin mushrooms grew in cow shit and he was on the alert for some of these golden topped beauties.

Low and behold he came upon a pile that had three big, fat mushrooms growing out of it.

"Hey there, beautiful darlings... You're gonna make my day a lot better." He knelt down to the ground and started picking them and putting them in his bag. He looked up to the sky.

"Well, God. Thanks for providing me with medication for my psychotic state." Dave walked over to a fallen tree and sat down bowing his head. "I'm just a piece of shit. Don't even know why you would even put up with me, God. I'm a disappointment to my folks. I can't keep a girl friend. I tore up our house. Why does this deep darkness overwhelm me? I just can't get out of this negative whirlpool... I know thinking this shit is wrong. Yet, I can't stop thinking it."

Dave slumped over sobbing uncontrollably.

"If there's such a thing as possession, this is it!" He looked up to the sky again. "God, help me!"

Mushroom Tea

Dave chopped up the last of the mushrooms and put them in a pot of dark black, boiling water. He straightened up the mess he made and put the coffee table back in place and the stuff back on it. After getting everything back in place he swept the floor while the mushrooms boiled out their potion. Once done he poured mushroom tea into a glass and drank the black, muddy concoction. He gags a bit as the slimy substance makes its way down his throat. It was time to crank up some rock and roll. With music blasting he sat on the couch grabbing the bong on the table. A bong was a smoking pipe that funneled the smoke through some water to cool the smoke down. This would enable the smoker to hold the smoke in longer. The water at the bottom of the pipe was brown colored from previous use and had its own peculiar smell. Smoking away he faded into a dream-like state.

A couple hours later Dave was bobbing his head up and down to the music and Jake walked in from work.

Jake said, "Hey, how's it going?"

"Great! Got some mushroom tea in there for ya."

"Mmmm... Sounds good!"

Moving on into the kitchen Jake grabbed the pot of tea and noticed the broken burner. "What the...? What happened to the burner?"

"I lost it, man. I'm sorry, I broke it."

"What?" Jake wheeled around to look Dave in the eye. "How'd you da...do that?"

"I got pissed. I did it with my hand..." Looking down at his banged up hand he said, "Busted up my hand a bit..." and pointing at the wall, "I screwed the wall up, too."

"Damn! How'd you put a hole in the wall?"

"With the chair."

"Da..da..damn it, Dave. We're gonna loose our da..da..deposit. What were you th..thinking?"

"I wasn't. Mary broke it off with me and I went into a rage."

Jake sipped his tea and made his way over to the couch. Dave handed him the bong and his Zippo lighter. Jake took a long hit, holds it and blows the remainder out.

Jake shaking his head said, "You need help, man. This ain't right. You can't go ta..tearing up the place every time a girl breaks up with you. Mary ain't the only girl in the world. There's more fish in the sea."

"I'm just tired of fishin'... It never works out for me. Women hate me." "Ca..ca..c'mon! Get over it... Here, take another hit."

Chapter 4

Zenduism

Dave had a problem keeping his cars on the road. Consequently when his VW bug threw a rod he was back to hitchhiking again. Dave was one to get back and forth from work no matter what it took. One day he was on the freeway with his arm out and thumb up coming home from work. It was rush hour traffic and a pickup truck swerved toward him and a passenger threw a half full beer can at him. Dave ducked the can but got sprayed. His middle finger shot up high.

"Screw you!!!", he said wiping the beer off his face.

Then someone drives by honking their horn and shaking their fist out their window yelling, "Get a job, ya long haired jerk!!!"

A cop approached in the distance. Dave pulled a joint out of his pocket, turned his back to the approaching officer and slipped it into his underwear. The cop drove on by without noticing.

Shortly after that a car pulled over to give him a ride. He made haste to meet it. Getting in the car he said, "Hey, thanks for the ride."

Zoe, a nicely rounded brunette in her 20s, responded, "No problem. Been there... Where ya going?" She wore a lacey top and tight bell-bottomed pants. She had that hippie look.

"Just outside of town…close to the fisherman's warf."

"I'm headed close to there, so I can get ya home."

"Thanks!" After some silence Dave said, "Hey, I got a joint if ya want to smoke it."

"Don't do it anymore."

"Well, you're better off anyway," Dave said with a chuckle. "I stashed it in my underwear."

Laughing Zoe said, "You got a point... You been drinking beer?"

"No... a redneck threw a beer can at me... Why don't you smoke anymore?" "Found something better."

"What's that?"

"I chant."

Dave looks at her quizzically. "What?"

"I'm into Zenduism... The more you chant the more benefits you get." "OK... whatever suits your fancy."

"Look. I'm going to a meeting now and it just happens to be close to where you live. You should check it out..." Dave was about to say no and Zoe said, "C'mon, if you don't like it... then nothing is lost... and ya might learn something."

"Aw, what the hell. I'll check it out. Can't hurt."

A few minutes later Dave found himself sitting on the floor in a living room with a fireplace and incense burning on the mantle. The room was filled with people; some sat on their knees; some were in a lotus position with legs crossed and a couple folks were sitting with one knee up and one leg tucked under.

The leader of the meeting, Zack, enthusiastically bounced up to the front of the room and said, "Welcome to all our followers. And..." looking at Dave, "to all our guests." Dave uncomfortably shifted his weight to his other butt-cheek in response.

Zack smiled broadly. "I'll give you a little introduction. In Zenduism we believe that the mind is the beginning of the world. We are here to develop and realize the full potential of the mind. Chanting is the way we prepare the mind for meditation. Chanting 'nam-myoho-renge-kyo' enables all people to perceive this Law in their own lives and to come into rhythm with it. By putting their lives in harmony with this Law, people can unlock their hidden potential and achieve harmony with the environment. Chanting will invoke protection and healing to the individual participating. We will begin with 'nam-myoho-renge-kyo'."

Zack settled down into the lotus position. In a deep melodic tone he sang, "Ah..uhmmm." It went on for a few seconds then he harmonically sang 'nam-myoho-renge-kyo'. Then the group all joined into a rhythmic and melodious 'nam-myoho-renge-kyo' over and over again. One person tapped out a beat on a small drum; another held their palms together swaying; another clapped to the beat; some ran their fingers through a string of beads; some had heads bowed and some were looking up with eyes closed. It reminded Dave of a rock concert where people were swaying and waving hands and dancing around but it was too religious to be a rock concert. Zack waved incense around as he chanted. 'Nam-myoho-renge-kyo' got faster and faster with musical overtones as some sang more guttural and some nasal.

Dave chanted ever-so-slightly and looked around with curiosity but, then, bows his head in subjection. It was an unusual concert; what it really needed to win Dave was drums, bass and an electric guitar wailing out some fast-fingered lead.

Could This Be It?

As Zoe drove Dave home some lightning flashes lit the darkened sky. Zoe with her usual enthusiastic smile said, "Hey, what'd you think?"

Dave tilted his head and said, "Not sure what to think. I have a hard time getting into what I don't understand."

"Well, I used to be a wreck. Into drugs and into a lot of trouble. I was into drugs because I had no peace. I was very depressed... even suicidal. But, since I've been chanting my life is so peaceful."

"How long you been chanting?"

"Two months."

"Well, I'm at one with the earth when I'm stoned. That's when I meditate. So, why should I change?"

A bright flash followed by a loud boom of thunder that made Zoe Jump. "Wow, that was loud..."

"That was a close one!" Dave pointed to a house coming up. "There's my place on the right. The one with the wooden porch."

Zoe pulled up in front of Dave's house and said, "You know, I chant two to three hours a day. The more I chant the more benefits I reap."

"Benefits?" "Yeah, like health and protection. You get in harmony with the planet and things start working in your favor." A sudden downpour made an instant roar on the car's roof.

"Looks like I may get wet!"

Dave leaned forward looking up into the sky at the same time as Zoe did. They both looked back to each other and laughed out loud.

Dave continued the ongoing conversation. "Well... I could play guitar 3 or 4 hours a day and I would get benefits. I would be a great guitar player. It wouldn't only benefit me but others who heard me. So, I would rather do that, than chant in some foreign language I don't understand. No offense, that's just the way I am." Laughing Zoe slapped Dave on the shoulder. "No offense taken. I like you. You seem like a good guy. And, I'm a pretty good judge of character." The weather shifted to a light rain.

They looked into each other's eyes until it got uncomfortable then Zoe said, "Hey, Dave. Maybe we could go out for a cup of coffee some time?"

"Sure. I'm game."

"Let me give you my number."

Pulling out a pad and pen from the glove box she wrote her name and number at the bottom of the sheet and tore it off. Folding up the piece of paper she handed it to him. A blinding light flashed with a loud thunder clap causing them to jump.

Zoe exclaimed, "You better get in before we get another burst."

"Good idea!"

"Hey, give me a call."

"Alright, I will."

Dave thrust the paper into his pants pocket and got out of the car.

Zoe waved "See ya."

"Until then... bye."

Dave closed the door and watched the car pull out, just standing there getting drenched. He pulled his keys from his pocket and the paper with her phone number fell out right next to the gutter barely touching the running water. Still watching the car Dave smiled and turned to go in the house.

Later Dave got ready for bed putting on a t-shirt and gym shorts. He grabbed his pants on the bed, pulled his keys out of his pocket and put them on his night stand. He then dug into the same pocket again. With a disparaging look he dug into the other pocket.

"Damn! Where the heck is that phone number!"

Frantically he looked on the bed, under the bed, around the room, in the living room, and under the cushions on the couch. He ran out to the porch looking on the ground. Tracing his footsteps back to where he was dropped off he scanned the sidewalk, the ground and the street. He put his hands on his head in despair. "You stupid idiot! You screwed it up again!"

While that was going on the folded piece of paper floated down the curb's gutter with the gushing water and spiraled down the culvert.

After giving up his search he went back to his bed and read Steppenwolf by Herman Hesse. The room was dark except for the small lamp by his bed. The joint he was smoking smoldered in the ash tray. He tossed the book on the night stand. "Well, God, here we are again, just You and me. Yep, stupid me. Screwed it up again. What else can go wrong." Dave grabbed the joint and took another long drag. "Don't know what to think about that chanting stuff but I'd better stick with You. You know, I could make up a bunch of Words to chant and it would do me as much good. How's this?"

Dave put his joint in the ashtray and sat up in his bed. He pulled his legs up in lotus position. Then he started rambling syllables. A bunch of syllables poured out of his mouth that actually sounded like a foreign language. With astonishment he said, "Dang. That sounds like French. I wonder if that's speaking in tongues... Naw, couldn't be. Too easy... Anyway, God, could you, please, put someone in my path that can show me what the hell is going on. Pardon the lingo. And, PS, sure could use some transportation." Dave picked up a spiral notebook beside the lamp and said, "Oh, yeah... in the name of Jesus Christ."

So, he picked up his pen and pad to write. He would write until he got sleepy enough to fall asleep. He had this goal to read from famous writers and then write. He started after a teacher in college encouraged him to turn in some poems, that he had written for class, for a poetry contest. Well, low and behold he won. That was his inspiration to learn to write. So, he prayed to God at the beginning of this quest, "God, if you teach me how to write someday I will write for You."

He was terrible at grammar so he would read and then write. When he had a question about punctuation he would keep it in mind until he found a similar sentence when reading. So he learned punctuation not by grammar but by observing how the master's punctuated. He still couldn't tell you the rules of grammar but his writing was getting pretty good. He also found that it was good therapy for his manic-depressive state. He determined he would follow this plan of reading and writing for 5 years. So by shear will and determination he learned to write. He liked writing poetry and short stories. Poetry helped him search for words that would rhyme. He would get a dictionary to see if his rhyming words fit. He started a book of poems called "Port Void Restrained". On this night looking through his dictionary he noticed that there weren't many "z" words, just a few pages. So, he decided he would write a poem with all the usable words that started with "z". This is what he came up with:

Zeta Freighter or Zed Bed or ZZZ

Zing zips for zealous zaibatsu
Zinc chameleon's charged zenith in tune
To zigzag a zesty zillion dollars.
Zooid's zone zooms through zero hour's zyme
To zoo zaney people into drunk buying zombies
Rather than zither pluck a zodiac
To zero in a zepplin's zephyr.

He used all the z's he could and was surprised at how short his poem was. He kept on thinking in a dream like fashion from the marijuana high. Thinking in this state was like hearing yourself talk to yourself, except often you would forget what you were saying. It wasn't too long before he faded off to sleep and more z's ensued.

Mom's Prayers

Dave stood next to his mom as she washed dishes. She grabbed a towel and dried off her hands and gave her undivided attention to her son. "The reason I asked you over is that your dad bought a motorcycle from a guy at work at a reasonable price. He thought you could use it to get around until you found something else."

"Oh, wow. That's great! Thanks!" Dave said. "So... there's other ways to get benefits."

"What?"

"Oh.. I met someone that chants and they say the more you chant the more benefits you get."

"Well, just don't forget about God."

"Don't worry, mom. I'm not into that. I'll always believe in God."

"You're always in our prayers. You know that, right?"

Dave gave mom a big hug. "You guys are always there through thick and thin. You know, I don't deserve parents like you."

Dave's mom smiled with a nod. "No, you don't", she chuckled and walked over to her purse to get a set of keys. She had an uncanny sense of humor at times. Handing the keys to him with a sheepish smile she said, "I would tell you to be good and have fun but I know you can't do both. So, have fun."

Dave took the keys and gave her another hug.

Chapter 5

Party to Oblivion

As Dave pumped gas into his 250cc motorcycle Mary pulled up to the tank on the opposite side. As she proceeded to get gas Dave spotted her and said, "Mary! Good to see you. It's been a while."

"Good to see you. When did you start riding a bike?"

"Just got it. My bug bit the dust."

Mary put the nozzle in and proceeded to pump gas. Awkwardly she obliged herself to speak. "Look, Dave. Just because we're not dating doesn't mean we can't be friends."

"Agreed." Dave topped his tank and put the handle back in the pump. Mary added "Hey, I'm going to a party tomorrow night. You want to come?"

"Sure. Where's it at."

"You know Sandra Beck?"

"No."

"She lives over on the corner of 11th and Oleander. It's the green house with a huge oak in the yard. You can't miss it."

"Sounds great."

"OK. And by the way... it's a drinkin' party. They don't smoke."

"No problem. I ain't much of a drinker but I love to party."

"OK. See ya then."

At the party a small group of people were talking and

drinking in the living room. Dave was sitting on the couch with Mary.

Slurring his words Dave said, "You know... I think we are pretty damn good for each other. Don't you think?"

Mary looked at him disappointedly. "I think you better slow down on your drinking."

"I'm pretty fucked up, aren't I?"

With a ring of the door bell Sandra, Mary's best friend, excused herself to see who was there. She opened the door and Shadow stood there grinning. Shadow looked pretty shady to her so she asked not so politely, "Who the hell are you?"

"I'm Shadow, a friend of Dave's."

"Oh, OK. Come on in."

Mary leaned over to Dave's ear. "Why'd you invite him."

He responded loudly, "It's a party ain't it."

Shadow found a spot next to Dave on the couch opposite Mary.

With pronounced slurring Dave said, "Shadow! Glad you could make it!"

"Thanks for the invite."

Almost incoherently Dave said in his sloppy stupor, "Hey man, I think I'm really getting drunk. I'm not a very good drunk."

"No shit. Could of fooled me," Shadow responded. "Yea. Maybe we better smoke a joint."

"You can't smoke here. They don't smoke dope."

"And, you call this a party?"

The door bell rang again and Sandra answered. A good-looking, clean-cut guy walked in. Sandra looked at Mary and said, "Hey, Mary, Jim's here."

Mary jumped up from the couch and gave Jim a hug and a kiss. Jim squeezed her in close and said, "Hey, baby."

"Hey, baby, let's talk in private..." Mary motioned to Sandra and Sandra moved in close for a more private word. Mary whispered, "Hey, could we borrow your bedroom?"

"Sure, go on back."

Jim and Mary made their way down the hall. Dave leaned over watching them go into a bedroom.

Shadow poked Dave in the side, chuckled and said, "Looks like he's going to get a piece of ass."

"Bull shit."

"She's pretty easy."

"Screw you!!!"

"That's what she did! Get over it, man!"

Dave jumped up from the couch stumbling over the coffee table. "Fucking coffee table. Damn shit." He stumbled on into the kitchen. "Fuck this shit!" Standing alone he desperately started looking around the room. Seeing a block with knives on the counter he grabbed a butcher knife. He just stood there with the knife in his right hand and staring at his left hand.

Walking into the kitchen Sandra observed the drama that was unraveling. She was a bit drunk by now and this kind of stuff disgusted her. "Go ahead and do it, you stupid idiot!!!" she yelled.

Dave looked up at her and said, "Fuck it!"

He brought the knife down hard on his wrist. Blood instantly gushed out from the wound. With a shocked look on his face he dropped the knife and slapped his hand on his wrist applying direct pressure to stop the bleeding. "Crap!"

he yelled instantly realizing how stupid he was to act like that.

Sandra in disbelief screamed, "What the hell's wrong with you!!!"

As people started crowding around the door to see what was happening Dave clutching his wrist to stop the blood flow said to Sandra, "Got any duck tape?"

"I do." She retrieved a roll of duct tape from a drawer and just stood their holding it. Dave's hands were tied as he held his wrist tightly. Blood was everywhere. Those observing were in shock and amazement at the unfolding scene.

Shadow walked in to see what was going on then hurriedly walked up to Dave and said, "You obviously need some help." He grabbed the roll from Sandra. "I'm going to start this tape and, when I say so, lift your hand so I can wrap this around tightly."

"OK."

"Go!"

Dave lifted his hand and Shadow quickly wrapped the tape tightly around Dave's wound while getting blood all over himself.

Dave with tears in his eyes said, "Oh, God, I've fucked up."

The wound stopped bleeding after a few wraps of the tape. Dave looked up seeing all the people staring at him. He dashed toward the door pushing people out of the way. Sandra started to go after him.

Shadow stuck his arm up to stop her and said, "Let him go. It's his damn life. We done all we can do."

Running out of the house Dave jumped onto his motorcycle. He started it up but had trouble pulling the clutch handle because his hand wouldn't close. He managed to pull the clutch by slightly bending the end of one finger and pulling back with his arm to get it to engage. He took off with a jolt ripping across the yard in first gear. As he headed down the street he managed to pull his arm back on the clutch to engage second gear. Tears streamed down his face. Pleading he said, "God. Please, save my life. Please, save my hand."

When he got to his house he dropped the bike in the middle of the front yard and ran into the house leaving the door wide open. He ran back to the bathroom, turned on the light, and looked at his horrified expression in the mirror. He started pulling the tape off to look at the damage. After a couple of unwinds a gush of blood shot out spraying the mirror.

"Oh, shit… I've fucked myself up." He yelled, "Damn it to hell!"

He quickly wound the tape back around his wrist to stop the flow. He laid down on the bathroom floor weeping and passed out.

Meanwhile back at the party Sandra was busy wiping blood off of kitchen floor and cabinets when Mary and Jim walked in.

Looking confused Mary said, "What happened?"

Sandra looking up said, "Your stupid shit friend decided he wanted to slit his wrist."

"Oh, my God. You mean Dave?"

"Yeah!"

"Where's he at? What happened?"

"The guy he was with wrapped his wrist with duct tape. Dave took off on his bike and his friend left muttering something about how he didn't want to get busted."

"That's crazy. Did you call for an ambulance?

"Hell no! Look, we got minors here you know."

"I got to go find him. He could die."

Jim looked dumbfounded as Mary ran out of the house.

At Dave's place Mary found him passed out laying on the bathroom floor in a pool of blood. She shook him to see if he was alive. "Dave, it's me, Mary." Dave groaned eerily, "Aughhhhh!!!"

She struggled to get him up. "C'mon get up."

He regained enough consciousness to help support his weight. She put one arm over her shoulder and with all her strength helped him get into her car.

Mary took him to the emergency entrance at the hospital, got him out of the car and hospital staff came running out to help bring him into the hospital.

Grim Consequences

Dave woke up in a hospital bed with his parents sitting next to him. His eyes opened and blinked and closed for a while, then opened again. Dave's mom stood while his dad remained seated. His mom caressed his hand. His other hand was on his chest with a cast on it, the fingers bent to a ninety degree angle.

"Hey, honey," his mom said tenderly.

"Hey."

There was a long silence then the doctor walked in. He walked up to the other side of Dave's bed. After looking at his clip board the doctor said, "How are you doing?"

"I'm hurting."

"You will be having a lot of pain for a while. It took us nine hours to put you back together. You severed all your tendons and a main artery. There was a major nerve that was partially cut. It should all grow back but you may have to deal with numbness the rest of your life. Tendons should heal up but it will take months of therapy to restore movement. But, I can't guarantee 100% recovery. You could have some loss of motion. You're lucky you didn't die."

"Who brought me in?" His dad said, "Mary found you and brought you in. I don't know how she managed but she got you here."

"I... I... don't remember."

Later that night when the hospital room was dark Dave squirmed on his bed due to a tremendous amount of pain. With tears in his eyes he grabbed the call button for the nurse and presses it.

Dave slammed his good hand on the bed. "I can't stand this." Rolling over slightly he yelled loudly, "Damn it! This hurts!" The nurse rushed in to give him pain medicine.

Recovery Time

Dave sat in a lawn chair on the front porch of his parent's home with a Dr. Pepper and a Bible on the small table next to him. Dave sipped on his favorite drink. His arm was in a sling with the cast on. His parent's lived in a typical middle class neighborhood.

Jed walked down the street toward Dave. He was clean cut, the military look, and was lanky and very tall. He was a Viet Nam vet that struggled with manic depression from time to time. When he saw Dave on the porch he waved. Dave waved back as Jed approached.

"Hey, I'm Jed. I live down the street. Moved in with my folks a couple of months ago."

"I'm Dave."

"Mind if I sit."

"Sure. I could use some company."

Jed sat down in the other lawn chair.

Dave said, "Man, your tall. How tall are you?"

"Six foot nine."

"Dang. You play basketball?"

"I hate basketball. Everybody asks me that."

"Sorry."

"No problem. I'm used to it...Hey, what happened to your arm?"

"I had an accident. Don't really want to talk about it."

"OK... Does it hurt?"

"It's awful."

Changing the subject Jed said, "Hey, was Shadow just here a while ago?" Dave said a little surprised, "Yeah. How do you know Shadow?"

"How does anyone know Shadow?"

"Yeah. Well... then, I guess... You want to smoke a joint?"

"Aw, man. You're a God send! How'd you know?"

Dave grins. "Association."

Jed grinned broadly as Dave pulled out a joint from his front shirt pocket. Dave said as he put the joint to his mouth, "Got a light?"

"Sure do!!!" Jed said as he pulled out a Zippo lighter and put the large flame close to his face.

"Quite a flame thrower you got there." Dave took a big draw to get it going and handed it to Jed. Jed took his turn then Dave blew his smoke out. There was a moment of silence while they were taking it all in.

Jed blew some smoke out and said, "So, I take it you moved back in with your folks, too." Jed handed the joint back to Dave.

"Yea, I can't work 'til this heals up. What do your parents do?"

Blowing the smoke out Jed said, "My dad's a preacher."

"No, shit... Sorry, pardon my lingo."

"No problem. Yeah, I'm a preacher's kid. Grew up with it."

"I heard about those preacher kids... pretty wild."

"Not that I don't believe. I do. I just don't think about it in the traditional way."

Dave held up the joint like a salute. "Know what you mean."

"Amen, brother."

More silence filled the air then Dave said, "Don't really feel like I know God very well. Know He's love. Can't tell you why I know it. I just do. That's probably the only thing that keeps me going."

"Cool."

"So, I'm going to start by reading the Bible and see where that goes", Dave said pointing at the Bible on the table. "I might even check out a church or two. I need to do something. Besides, Mom's been trying to get me to go for a long time."

Physical Therapy

Dave sat across from a physical therapist at a table. His cast had been removed and he was healed up enough for therapy. His fingers were frozen in the shape of the cast with fingers bent. They seemed impossible to move. The therapist massaged his hand.

Grabbing Dave's fingers the therapist said, "OK. I'm going to stretch out your fingers. We have to do this or you will lose motion in your fingers. You will have to be determined and push and stretch and exercise your hand daily. It will be very painful."

"OK. Let's do this thing."

The therapist stretched his stiff fingers about half way.

Dave screamed "Aughhhhh" as tears ran down his face.

Hell, Fire and Brimstone

Dave decided he needed to check out a church. He was still going through days of depression and was just plain sick of it. There was a church in walking distance and he decided to check it out. He was late and the sermon was already going on. He snuck in and sat in a pew in the back. The preacher was preaching away but noted his entrance. The church was half full with mostly older folks and some families. They were clean cut, prim and proper. He was the only long haired hippie in the congregation.

The preacher pounded on the pulpit. "God hates sin. And, we're all sinners. So, it's time to change your ways. People doping and messing around have got to change. All these hippies running around shows that we're in the last times. And, I'm telling you now." He looked Dave straight in the eye. "Long hair on a man is sin!!!"

An older guy in the same pew looked at Dave with disgust. Dave shrunk down in the pew waited a little bit then quietly got up and left. Some people close by glared at him as he left.

Chapter 6

From the Frying Pan to the Fire

Couple of months later Dave sat in the living room at his parent's house with a bag of dope on the coffee table. They were at work so he could enjoy a smoke inside. His hand was pretty functional except it was partially numb. Shadow sat with him with a bottle of whisky in a brown paper bag. They were sharing hits off of a joint.

After taking a hit off the joint Shadow said, "Looks like you're healing up real good."

"Yep, I got all the movement back in my hand. The only thing is that half my hand is numb. Probably have to deal with that the rest of my life."

"Glad to hear you're doing well... I thought you were going to die." He grabbed his bottle and said, "Hey, let's celebrate. Got some good whiskey, here." Shadow twisted the cap off and took a swig. "Mmmm... Good stuff!" He handed the bottle for Dave.

"Aw, I don't know. Not that big on alcohol."

"Aw, man. A swig or two won't hurt."

"OK." Taking the bottle he took a sip.

"C'mon. You can do better than that."

Dave took a bigger swig. It wasn't too long before the bottle was empty and Dave was obviously drunk.

Now, was the time for Shadow to make his move. "Hey,

man, I got something I want you to help me with. I got some blank company checks. I've cashed a few and it's been easy money but I don't want them to get suspicious. Could you go in and cash this one. You can have half the money."

"I don't know. I don't feel right about doing that. Besides, I'm a little tipsy."

"Aw, c'mon. It's just this once. I know ya ain't been working. I'm sure you could use a little money."

"I don't know."

"C'mon, man. It's in and out. Simple."

"OK. I guess."

"OK. Let's go."

Dave put the bag of marijuana under the couch and left with Shadow. Shadow pulled up to a drug store with Dave. Dave went into drug store, walked up to the counter and held the check out to the cashier.

"I want to cash my payroll check."

"Let me see your ID."

Dave pulled out his driver's license and handed it to the cashier. The cashier looked closely at the picture then eyed Dave.

"I will need to get this cash from the safe in the back. Excuse me."

He took the driver's license with him. It seemed to be taking forever and Dave started to get nervous.

The cashier came back with money in hand and said, "OK. Could you sign the back of this check."

Dave signed the check. The cashier very slowly started counting out the cash to him. As he counted a cop car pulled up and two cops walked into the store. Shadow started his car and drove away.

The cashier looked up and took the money back. Dave looked up at him quizzically and turned around to see the cops standing behind him. It was his good ole friends, Officer Ward and Jimbo.

Officer Ward grinned broadly. "Well, well, well...if it's not our favorite foe, Dave Brinkley. Your busted, son. And, it gives me great pleasure to read you your rights. You ain't getting out of this one this time."

Jimbo turned Dave to the counter and clamped on the hand cuffs.

Defense Attorney

Mr. Fredericks sat at his desk in his office. Dave's mom sat in a chair in front of the desk. Dave's dad paced the floor. Mr. Fredericks looking at a document said, "His bail is set at $50,000. It would take $5,000 to get him out." Dave's dad froze in his steps. "Damn... How can he be so stupid...We can't afford that."

Looking at George Mr. Fredericks added, "The good part is that the judge allowed me to be his court appointed lawyer, so the state will pay. The bad is that they've indicted him for 13 counts of passing a forged instrument which is a felony."

"What! I thought it was just one."

"That's true but their witness thinks he did them all."

Bettye sobbed putting her hands to her face. George sat down next to her and put his arm around her.

Shadowy Jail

Dave sat on a bench in the county jail with another inmate, John, inside the large recreation area of that cell block. The room had several benches and picnic type tables that were melded into the concrete floor and welded. There was a tube TV mounted high in the corner of the room. Some inmates stood in groups talking, some sat joking, some were playing cards and some stared at the TV.

A loud thud rang out and inmates rushed over to the corner of the room yelling loudly encircling two men. One of the men pounded the other with a sock with a bar of soap inside. The victim's nose gushed out blood and his lip was split open. He curled up in a ball with his arms over his head shielding the blows. Soon the guards ran in to break it up. They escorted the two out of the cell block. John chuckled, "It's amazing how resourceful you can get here. Turning a sock and a bar of soap into a weapon. Ingenious."

Dave responded, "Is that what I've got to look forward to?"

"Just don't be an asshole and you'll be fine. Stay quiet and mind your own business. And, if someone pisses you off let it go and move on. They'll test you. If you're liked they'll take care of you. If you're not, it's a living hell." John takes a long drag off his cigarette. "Hey, what you in for?"

"Passing a forged check. A friend of mine, Shadow, talked me into it." "You're kidding me? I know Shadow."

"No shit?"

"Yeah. A few years ago we were in the same cell. He was in on a possession charge... So, they're still calling him Shadow."

"What do you mean?"

"That got started here. He was outside in the yard and noticed his shadow was on the other side of the fence. He went around saying, he might be in jail but his shadow was free. We all started calling him shadow after that. Guess it stuck."

"Small world."

"It's smaller in here."

Settling In

After being incarcerated for a couple weeks Dave got into a routine of reading the books made available on the daily cart. He was no longer concerned about getting his ass whipped. Most people there liked him and defended him. He sat on his haunches on the floor against the wall in his cell reading Civil Disobedience by Henry David Thoreau. Tom, his other roommate, leaned against the wall on the top bunk looking at a magazine with his feet dangling.

John entered and seeing Dave on the floor said, "Hey, Dave, I told you that you could sit on my bunk while I'm away."

The jail was crowded and there were more people than bunks so there were many who had a mattress under a bunk. Dave slept under the bunk.

"Sure, thanks."

Tom in his usual manner said, "Speak for yourself. No one's touching my bunk."

John said grinning, "No one wants to touch your bunk, you dirty piece of shit."

Tom laughed, "I love you, too."

"Hey, Dave, I'm gonna call you 'the scholar that came out

from under the bunk'. You're reading all the time. How many books have you read?"

"Three so far."

Dave was still onto his goal of reading and writing. He had plenty of time to do that. He was thrilled when reading Henry David Thoreau's "Civil Disobedience". Inspired, he wrote a short essay he called "Uncivil Obedience". It reflected some of the atrocities he encountered while in jail. His cellmates got to hear bits and pieces of it. Some would copy portions of it and share it with others. This helped him gain respect amongst the prisoners in his ward and they made sure no one gave him a hard time. One of the poems he wrote gained popularity. It went like this:

Pushed Side to Side

Officer Blue stripped me off the street.
My rights were denied for the offense I tried.
Blue said, "Son, you're in for a while. Jail's your new bride"
I said, "I'll see you in divorce court.
Hey, Blue, let me smoke your short."

Look side to side, check the back door
For if you haven't a chance they'll get you for more
Without a dime for a call or a chance to score.
Officer Blue read me my rights.
He stripped the clothes off my back, looked up my crack.
I think he was looking for a railway spike
'Cause he asked me if I had any tracks.

"Hey, Blue, I'll give you the facts. I smoke my dope but I don't shoot smack."
Pushed side to side, lock the only door.
If you come in late you'll sleep on the floor.
Two to a blanket and a cold in store.

Thomas Jefferson was in my cell, too much bail.
He was charged with treason for his written reason.
He was busted at a "T" party in Boston.
"Inciting a right" he said, "I was only teasin'."
Guilty until proven innocent; don't care if you know the president.
Reds, whites and blues will get you ten
And Thomas Jefferson's sent to the pen.
I guess, I'll find a new best friend.

There were several more verses to his poem but that was the gist. The main thing was that his reading and writing continued to persist.

Enough Is Enough, Time to Pray

Dave had been getting increasingly more depressed as the weeks sluggishly went by. Thoughts of suicide were starting to swarm his head. He was getting a little touchy. His good sense of humor had all but gone. This was a very dangerous state to be in. All he had to do is piss off the wrong guy and he would get his head pounded.

One night, when all was quiet and everybody slept, Dave was laying on his back on his mattress staring at the bottom of John's bunk. His face was about six inches from the metal bunk above.

Closing his eyes he whispered, "God, I'm tired of this shit. Six weeks and I still don't know a thing. I'm really getting depressed about this. I swear, if I don't know something soon I'm going to kill myself. I can't take this shit any longer."

In an instant Dave was vividly aware of God's presence. In his heart of hearts he knew that when he went to court he would be set free. He couldn't tell you how or why but he knew that he knew it was God. This was the first time in Dave's life that he got an immediate answer from God to a prayer. Tears of joy started flowing from his eyes. "Thank you, Father. Thanks!!! That's all I needed to know."

The next morning John and Tom sat on their bunks. Dave pulled himself out from under the bunk, stretched, and sat on the bunk beside John.

Dave said scratching his belly, "Wow. I didn't even hear the doors open. I was out of it... I had a wild thing happen last night."

"What's that."

"I prayed last night and got an immediate answer."

Tom laughing out loud said, "Yeah, right. You're mind does crazy stuff in here."

John scowled at Tom, "Shut up, Tom... Go on, Dave."

"I told God I had to know what was going to happen... I can't explain it. But, I knew immediately that I would be released on the day of the trial."

Tom burst out with laughter that was heard at the end of the hall. "Now, I've heard it all. You done got religious on us." He laughed some more.

"Well, I know it sounds crazy but I know that I will absolutely be released that day."

Tom shook his head. "Is this jail or an insane asylum?"

A few days later in the recreation area the usual crowd was milling around, talking in groups or watching TV. Dave sat on a bench reading a book.

John walked up to Dave with a book in his hand. "Hey, glad you're getting out and about more."

"I'm not as paranoid as I used to be."

"I got something for ya from the book man." He handed him a Gideon's Bible.

"Alright, a Bible. When do I have to have it back?"

"It's yours. They were giving 'em away."

"Did you get one?" "Don't have the patience for that... but... you could always share what you're learning."

Dave devoured his Bible starting from the New Testament. He wanted to read it in the past and kept putting it off but now he had plenty of time.

Death and the Devil

One night down the hall from Dave's cell an inmate, Buster, sat on his bunk with an inmate on each side while another sat on the floor. John stood in the opening of the door while others were crowded around listening in.

One of the inmates inside the cell yelled out in a most religious and sarcastic way, "Praise the Lord. We got a prophet, here."

The inmates listening in were chuckling and nudging each other. Dave walked up to John to find out what was going on.

John said, "Hey, check out our new resident. He's telling everybody how he murdered a guy because God told him to."

"OK... I want to check this guy out."

Dave walked through the crowd into the cell.

Tom was ready to jump on this opportunity. "Hey, here's the scholar that came out from under the bunk." Then, he very sarcastically said, "He reads the Bible all the time. What's your take on this guy."

Dave questioned Buster, "So, you say God told you to kill someone?"

Buster responded, "That's right. God took me over. Then, I don't remember the details because I was God's instrument. But, the next thing I knew, I was standing over the dude with a knife in my hand and blood was gushing out of his throat."

"How do you know it was God?"

"Only God has that kind of power over a person."

"Do you believe in the Bible."

"Of course, I do."

"Then you know there is a God and the devil."

"Of course."

Dave motioned to sit down next to Buster and an inmate scooted over for him. "God is good and the devil is bad. That I know. So, you have to determine whether killing that person was from God or the devil... I believe the third eye, right here..." he points to the middle of his forehead between his eyes. "I may be wrong... but I believe this is where the receptor is for receiving spiritual communication. Now in your case, you have to determine which spirit was talking to you. I've been possessed a couple of times. I lost total control. Jesus Christ didn't go around killing people. I read a verse a few days ago... I think it's in Hebrews... It said the devil has the power of death."

Buster looked at Dave bewilderedly. "Crap. That's what the Bible says?" "Yep. Black and white. Death is not from God. If you weren't conscious when you did it, that's possession. God doesn't possess. The devil possesses." "Shit. Not sure what to think, now."

"I would ask God to forgive you... then start over. I've had to do that plenty of times."

"OK. I'm sorry. This is embarrassing."

"Get over being embarrassed. With God you can get over it and move on." Dave patted Buster on the shoulder and got up and stepped outside the cell next to John.

John shook his head and said, "I can't believe you, Dave. Maybe all that Bible reading is doing some good."

"Don't know about that. Been pretty frustrated reading it at times. At the end of the book of Revelation it warned against anyone adding to or taking away from those words. Shit, I'm guilty of that... Now, I feel like I got to start all over... Anyway, the verse that the devil has the power of death helped me in this situation... that verse was clear."

"So, you're gonna start over... after finishing the book?"

"Well, I started in the New Testament so it's not like I'm finished. I figure it's got to be more pertinent to us now than the Old Testament. It's not like I understood much but even bits and pieces of truth has gotta help."

John nodding his head said, "Hey, I heard you go to court Wednesday." "Yep, I'm getting out that day."

"You sound pretty convinced."

"I am."

Judgment Day

Dave and Mr. Fredericks sat at a table in court in front of the judge and behind them sat his parents in a partially filled court room. The judge faced them looking down and flipping through some pages.

Judge Thompson looked up and said, "The State of Texas vs. David Brinkley. Mr. Brinkley has been charged with 13 counts of passing a forged instrument. Does he understand the charges?"

Mr. Fredericks stood and responded, "He does, your honor."

"In reviewing the case it has been brought to my attention that the check that the defendant signed has a different signature than the rest of the checks. Thus, the court has decided to reduce the charge to a misdemeanor for passing the single forged check. How does the defendant plea to this charge."

"The defendant pleas guilty, sir." Mr. Fredericks replied.

"Then, I would like the defendant to rise for sentencing."

Dave looked at Mr. Fredericks. Mr. Fredericks nodded and Dave stood up. Judge Thompson read from a document. "For the misdemeanor of passing a forged instrument the court sentences you with 90 days in prison to be served in the county jail. Since you just served your ninetieth day in jail this week you will get time served and be released at midnight tonight."

Dave turned to his lawyer and gave him an exuberant hug. He then turned to his parents with broad smile. They were happy and relieved.

Chapter 7

Job Opportunities?

Dave and Jed sat on the front porch smoking a joint. Jed thumbed through the daily paper.

Jed said, "Good to have you back, man... Hey, how come they didn't shave your head."

"They don't do that 'til you been convicted."

"Don't know if I could have handled jail that long."

"God came through for me on that... I was getting suicidal."

Jed said, "I get suicidal a lot. War does a trip on your head."

"I know. Depression is a bummer." Dave took a drag on the joint and handed it to Jed and he sat it down in the ashtray and continued to thumb through the paper.

Dave said, "Know anything about signs and wonders?"

"I guess it's about God's amazing timing of events."

"Well... I read 13 books while in jail. I got a 90 day sentence and got out of jail at the end of the 13th week which was Friday the 13th. When they gave me my possessions back I only had 13 cents."

"Weird."

"I know the number 13 seems to be an unlucky number however I don't believe in luck. Maybe this is to signify that even though I did stupid stuff, God's got my back."

"You shouldn't do stupid stuff anyway."

"True. But, getting talked into trying to cash that check was the number one on the stupidity charts."

Jed folded his paper over to look at an ad a little closer. "Hey, here's something in the want ads... It says, 'Help wanted. Need dependable people looking for a career that will enhance their lives and the lives of others. Great opportunity to travel around the country with all expenses paid. If interested contact...' Then, it gives the number."

"It's probably sales. And, I don't like sales. But... I do need a job."

"Well, I'll give 'em a call. See what happens. I would love to travel and make a living, too."

"I'd just love to make a living. My old boss would love to have me back but work's been too slow lately."

Later Jed called the number on the ad and they invited them to come to a meeting that would fill them in on the job. They reassured him that it was not sales.

So Jed and Dave made their way into the heart of the city to check it out. They got a little lost and had to check the city map a couple of times. They found the house; it was an older style house in a nicely kept, but dated, neighborhood.

Inside were rows of folding chairs with room for a speaker up front and a old tube TV to one side on a stand with a huge 3/4" video tape deck on the shelf underneath.

Dave and Jed found a seat. A dozen or so people of different backgrounds were seated in the main living room; there were some in business attire, a gal that looked like a housewife, a Mexican with tattoos, some casually dressed but neat, and a couple more hippie-types.

Dennis bounced up to the center of the room by the TV. "Welcome, friends. I am here to introduce to you an opportunity that will empower you to make the world a better place to live, an opportunity to bring all races together and unite as one family. We will start with a short introductory video and then we will show you what is available through this wonderful organization."

Dennis pressed play on the video tape deck on a shelf under the TV. The picture rolled when it started with lines of noise indicating a wrinkle in the tape. The video stabilized and started with MUSIC and city shots. It showed the poverty and depravity of the world then proposed a society without hate and fear; a society based on brotherly love and helping each other. It played for about 10 minutes. As the credits rolled Dennis stepped back up to the front and turned the audio down on the TV. "There you have it. This is your chance to do something about this world and make a positive difference. We don't expect you to make a decision now. But, what we will do is show you in detail what the Rectification Church is all about. This Saturday we will be taking a bus load of interested people to our lovely ranch in Oklahoma to spend a week with us and see how we operate. There you will learn more about the Heavenly Principle that we operate to bring peace, joy, and enlightenment to mankind. We want you to be able make an informed decision. So I hope you will join us. I will be available to answer any questions. So, this ends the formal part of this meeting."

Some people made their way to the door to leave while others went up to the front to ask Dennis questions. Jed and Dave stayed seated and observed.

Dave leaned over to Jed and softly said, "I didn't think this was going to be some sort of religious thing."

Jed shrugged his shoulders, "Well, they were quoting Bible in the video so it can't be too bad."

"I suppose."

"Look. I see it as an opportunity to get out of town for a while and see how other people live. It can be like a vacation. We don't have to buy into it."

"OK. What the heck. As long as I'm not letting someone talk me into doing something stupid."

They both laughed.

Rectification Church

Eight people traveled in a passenger van on the trip to Rectification Church Family Ranch. It was about a 10 hour trip. The driver had to stop at the property gate to open it up. It was under lock and key. The ranch was well kept with a moderately large vegetable garden with a couple of folks weeding; they stood up and waved as the van drove by. The van pulled up to a country farm house. It was a fairly large house, single story with a long porch on the front. There was another van already parked in the gravel lot where they pulled up. Jed and Dave stood and stretched right where they were seated as the other passengers made their way off the bus. Jed had to stoop because of his height. As they came off the bus, some stretching and yawning, one of the ranch's staff, Debra, walked briskly up to greet the group.

Smiling brilliantly Debra said, "Welcome everybody. My name is Debra and I am here to show you around and get you orientated. Come on in. I'm sure you're hungry. We'll get you fed first up." The group followed Debra into the farm house.

After dinner they spent some casual time talking in the living room and on the porch which was the whole front of the house with chairs and small tables for fellowship. After some time hanging out they were shown their rooms. There were a couple of large rooms with some bunk beds, one for women and one for men. The men in the group settled in putting their clothes in the shared closets and some just putting their bags by their bunk, content with just working from their bag for their clothes and toiletries. Some of the men quickly laid down on their bed while others were putting away belongings getting ready to bed down.

One of the staff, Jim, poked his head in the door. "Hey, guys. We got a busy schedule in the morning. Breakfast is at 7:30 and then you will be into your first session… In other words, it's time for bed. OK. Lights out at 10:30. Hall light will be on so you can find the bathroom."

Some grumbled in the ranks as they hurried up with their things and hopped in bed.

Despairingly Jed said, "7:30? I need my beauty rest."

Dave responded, "You may need rest but it won't help on the beauty."

A few chuckles came from the group.

Jim poked his head in the door again. "Alright! Here goes the lights. All ready?"

After a couple of groans and nods Ben turned the light off and shut the door. There was silence. Then, out of the blue came a loud "ppfft" from a fart. Everyone ignored the blatant interruption. A long "ppppfffftt" burst out from another part of the room. A couple of chuckles were held back with difficultly. Then, Felipe, a large man of Mexican descent said, "Hey, man. It's the beans, man. I can't hold my beans."

More laughter came from the guys. Then, another fart blasted.

Donny said laughing, "I'm laughing so hard, I'm farting."

The room broke out in hilarious laughter.

Jed wiped his tears from his face. "I'm crying."

Dave said barely getting his words out from the laughter, "You're farts are making me cry, too."

The laughter was rolling in waves now.

Dave continued, "Now, I know what it means to cast out foul spirits." A final crash of laughter rolled in like a wave pounding a beach.

The next morning a group of people walked into a living room with theater style seating and a TV on a stand up front. Some were quiet while others were chatting as the guests made their way in. One of the staff directed Dave and Jed to their seats.

As soon as everyone was settled in Dennis briskly walked up, center stage. "Well, we've got a lot to cover so let's get started. We are thrilled that you have all come to join us and have the desire to help others. The Rectification Church is rapidly growing and bringing people to spiritual enlightenment all over the world. Our founder, Rev. Moo Gon Lee, converted to Christianity at a very young age. As a young man Jesus appeared to him and asked him to continue his work."

Dave looked over to Jed and Jed returned the look. Dave shrugged his shoulders and turned back to listen.

"He fervently studied the Bible and developed the Heavenly Principle. The video you are about to see is Rev. Lee with subtitles. So, get comfortable and enjoy the Heavenly Principle." Dennis hit play on the large video deck and signaled Jose who stood by the door. Jose lowered the lights. The picture rolled from a wrinkle in the tape as the video started and then Rev. Lee started speaking in Korean with subtitles underneath. Dave shifted in his chair uncomfortably more interested in watching Dennis as he walked to a chair at the side of the room.

Making Friends

That evening after dinner was a beautiful orange sunset. Jose sat in a rocking chair on the front porch. Jed and Dave were sitting in lawn chairs with him.

Jose shifted his gaze off the sunset to Dave. "So what do you think?"

Dave said, "Well, it makes sense. I'm glad that they use scripture. So far sounds really good."

"What about you, Jed."

Shifting uncomfortably in his chair Jed said, "It's all good. But, my dad's a preacher and it would kill him if I defected to another ministry."

Jose nodded. "Family is important but eventually you have to do what God wants you to."

"I suppose."

Dave piped in, "How long you been with this group?"

"It's been a little over a year, now."

Jed shifted his chair to face Jose more directly. "What'd you do before?"

"I was a truck driver.... I carried bricks inside of bricks from Mexico, man. You know?"

Dave grinned broadly. "I know exactly what you mean. I've scored a brick or two from Mexico myself." A larger quantity of marijuana often came in kilo sized bricks. They were compressed and compacted so they could carry more in smaller spaces when crossing the border.

Jose winked and said, "Wouldn't mind a little puff. It's been a while."

Jed said, "Hey, I got some in my bag. Is there a place we can do it?"

Dave did a double take. "You brought some?"

"Sure, we're on vacation. What's a vacation without it."

Pointing out toward the woods Jose said, "There's a nice little spot in the woods past that field we can go to. We've got enough time for a quick one."

"Let me go get my stash. I'll be right back."

Jed hopped up quick to go fetch it. Then, they took a stroll to the woods. After a while they came back laughing and cutting up. It was twilight and getting close to time for the evening session.

They learned more in the next video about unity and tapping into the universal spirit of love. Many Bible verses were quoted along the way to prove the points Rev. Lee made. He taught on God's purpose for man, the fall of man, and the process of restoration.

The next day Dave sat on the porch with a married couple, Frank and Brandy. Dave was still mulling over what they were learning in the sessions. It really sounded good but he wanted to be sure. "So, what do you guys think of this movement?"

Frank responded, "It makes sense. We've talked to Dennis about joining. He informed us that we would have to separate for a while for some sort of purification process then Rev. Lee would remarry us."

Dave frowned a bit. "That's sort of weird."

Brandy added, "Yea, but it makes sense. We need to learn The Heavenly Principle without distraction."

The Rectification Church was known for mass weddings performed by Rev. Lee himself. It was for those who have spiritually matured and become one with God by way of The Heavenly Principle. Dave still had a hard time understanding what that really was. Maybe because he still needed to mature and become rectified. However, about the marriage thing they didn't tell them after their cleansing process that they would pick who they were to marry and most of the time it was a different person than they were married to when they joined. It was under the guise that they wanted you to have the best suited spouse.

Cry in My Beer Prayer

One night after a session the staff and guests went out to an open field close to the ranch house where a camp fire was going strong. They gathered around the campfire in a circle and sat on stumps and logs that were placed around it. One of the staff members was poking logs in the fire with his walking stick to stir up some flame. People were chatting for a while enjoying the warm light and flames.

After a few minutes Dennis stood and addressed the group, "Let's all stand and hold hands." And, guess what? The talking stopped and they stood and held hands.

Dennis continued, "OK. Let's take some time to pray and lift our cares to God. Linda, would you start?"

Linda, one of the staff, bowed her head. Many in the group bowed their heads in unison. Dave continued to look around then bowed his head.

Linda prayed, "Oh, God. We are so sorry for all the terrible things that are going on in this world. There's so much sickness and poverty. We're so sorry. Lord, help those who are in need. Amen."

Dave looked around during the pause.

Another staff member said, "Please, God, there's so much evil going on today." At this point tears started to roll down his face and his voice began to break. "It's awful, all the drugs, rape, and murder. Children are hungry. The evil is overwhelming. May we bring some light to those poor tortured souls. Please, help us to get the word out that they can be rectified back to you, God."

Most of the guests were not confident enough to pray out loud in front of everybody. So some silence ensued. Brandy was the first to speak up while sobbing. Some of her religious upbringing came through. "Father, we are so vile before you. We repent of our awful deeds. We like sheep are gone astray. We're sinners, all of us. Please, don't let us perish."

After another longer pause Dave looked around a little more intently. He never liked cry-in-my-beer country music and all this sobbing and feeling sorry was getting to him. And, the whole sad mood was just plain distasteful. Then, a sheepish, cheeky grin spread across his face and he began to pray. "What's happening, God?" Several of Dave's new friends did their best to hold back their chuckles. "I just want to thank You for all the friends I've made while being here. I know you're the God that makes life enjoyable. We've had some good times. Thanks for the laughter we've had together, in the name of Jesus Christ." That prayer shifted the mood from sadness to gladness. The group was dead silent until it was almost uncomfortable.

Dennis piped in, "OK, now, enough for one night. We best get ourselves some rest for another great day of learning."

The Turning Point

They came to their last full day at the ranch. Dave and Jed walked out onto the porch and sat in a couple of lawn chairs. Dave blew out a long breath with a furled brow and looked at Jed. "I was hooked, line and sinker, until... what I just heard."

Jed responded with a quizzical look.

Dave explained, "I don't buy it that Rev. Lee is the lord of the sacred venture and that he is taking the place of Jesus Christ. Who can take the place of Jesus Christ?"

Jed nodded.

Dave put his finger to his chin and continued, "He said Jesus wasn't really coming back. My knowledge of the Bible is not extensive but I remember reading distinctly that Jesus Christ was coming back in the same way that he left."

Jed nodded saying, "Yea, I think I recall something about him descending from heaven."

Jose emerged from the house smiling then he got serious after seeing the seriousness on Jed and Dave's faces. He sat down next to them. "What's with you guys?"

Jed shrugged his shoulders. "Not much."

Jose shook his head. "Somethin's up. I smell it."

Jed said forcing a smile, "Got a lot to chew on."

Still troubled about the last session Dave said, "Jose, is there a Bible around somewhere? I want to look something up."

"Sure. Just a second." Jose dashed into the house and searched a bookshelf then looked in a couple of desk drawers where he found a Bible. He went back outside and handed it to Dave.

Dave flipped through the pages clumsily, not quite sure where to find the passage. "It's in the New Testament somewhere."

In an attempt to help Jed said, "Most Bibles have a small concordance in the back."

"Good idea."

Dave flipped to the back of the Bible and looked up quizzically. "Don't know what to look for."

Jed said, "Look up descend."

Dave fingered through a few more pages. "Descend... descend... Here it is." Dave ran his finger through the references. "It says t-h 4:16. What's t-h?

Jed chuckled, "Thessalonians you duffus."

"Where's it at?"

Jed reached out for the Bible. "Here, give me that thing."

Upon receiving it Jed flipped through some pages. "I think it's somewhere around here... Yea, here it is." He turned another page and ran his finger down the verses. Jose leaned over to read along.

Jed read, "It says, 'For the Lord himself shall descend from heaven with a shout, with the voice of the archangel, and with the trump of God: and the dead in Christ shall rise first'."

Dave was thrilled. "There it is! The Lord himself shall descend. He is coming back. That's an out and out contradiction from what Rev. Lee is teaching." Jose leaned back shaking his head. He walked to the edge of the porch and stared out at the fields. He turned back to the guys. "My mama taught me to only trust the Bible."

Dave nodded. "She taught you right! Can I borrow this." He pointed to the Bible.

"No problem."

The Power of One Biblical Truth

Dave stood with a group outside the house in the yard with the Bible opened. Frank and Brandy were among the handful of folks listening to Dave. They had been considering joining the group but were still unsettled about separating; however, they were willing to do so if it were God's will.

Dave was wrapping up what he learned from the Bible, "And that's what it says in the Bible. Jesus is coming back himself. See the verse before says 'the coming of our Lord'."

Brandy looked at Frank. Frank responded, "I don't know. That is what it appears to say."

Dave continued, "I found another one in the first chapter of Acts. The angels said when he ascended into heaven that he would come back in the same manner." He turned to the page, he had marked in Acts. "It's in Acts 1:11." He opens the Bible so Frank and Brandy can read along. Reading he said, "Which also said, Ye men of Galilee, why stand ye gazing up into heaven? this same Jesus, which is taken up from you into heaven, shall so come in like manner as ye have seen him go into heaven." He looked them straight in the eye. "See... he's coming back the same way he left."

Brandy went from a concerned look to a relieved look. "Well, that settles it for me. I guess, the Bible has to be our standard."

The others in the group shook their heads in agreement. One gentleman patted Dave on the back and thanked him.

Parting Words

Dave and Dennis sat on their bums near the edge of the pond. Dennis was making his final pitch to Dave to join the group. "I see great potential in you, Dave. I really think you should consider joining up with us."

Dave respectfully responded, "Well, I've got to tell ya. I was sold until Rev. Lee said Jesus wasn't coming back... The Bible says he is coming back."

"OK..." Dennis was silent for a moment looking at the pond. "See that moss on the pond."

"Uh-huh."

"What's that look like to you."

"A cross."

"That's a sign. God wants you to do the right thing."

"That may look like a cross but so do the power lines. I've got to stick with what the Bible says… Besides, that moss was there before we started having this conversation."

"What if you're wrong?"

"What if I'm right? Or… I should say what if the Bible is right? Those verses I found are clear and simple. If you want to contradict what is pure and simple then, I hate to say it, but I think you're anti-Christ."

Dennis looking offended said, "I'm very sorry you feel that way."

Later that day after lunch a group of people stood around the van. Frank and Brandy came out of the house with their bags in hand. Jose was hugging some of the staff members.

Jose said, "I'm gonna miss you guys."

Dennis patted him on the back. "I really think you should stay."

"I gotta do this... for me. I appreciate all you did for me but it's time to move on."

More hugs and kisses as the group got on the bus. The bus drove off as people waved. It turned out most those that came out were thinking seriously of joining but after Dave shared what the Bible said they all with one accord decided against it. It was a powerful moment for Dave seeing how God's Word could make a difference in people's lives.

Chapter 8

Back to Work, Back to Jail and Back to God

Dave ended up getting his old concrete construction job back when the work picked up. He was always a hard worker and the company valued him as an employee. It was Dave's first week back. As a cement truck was getting into position to pour mud into several of the culvert forms Dave talked to Shadow and put a bag of dope in his tool pouch. They shook hands and Shadow walked off. Then, Clyde, the foreman, walked up to Dave.

Dave shook Clyde's hand. "Hey, thanks for hiring me back. I really needed the work."

"No problem. I would of hired you sooner if we had the work. You staying for the Christmas party?"

Dave chuckled, "Never miss a party."

As Shadow drove off another car made a sudden dip into the yard and slammed on the brakes with dust flying.

The nice looking gal sticks her head out of the window. "Hey, you!" She pointed at Dave. "Why didn't you ever call me?"

Dave leaned over to have a closer look. "Is that Zoe?"

"Yeah, it's Zoe. Where you been?" Zoe got out of the car and walked over to Dave.

"Hey, I would of called you but I lost your number."

Teasing she said, "Likely excuse."

"What you been up to? Still going to those Zendu meetings?"

"No, I'm into the real deal now… I'm into the Bible."

"No shit. Now, I could get into some of that."

"I'll hook you up. Look, I gotta get to my folks house. Christmas eve, you know. Let's exchange numbers. I won't loose yours.", she said laughing.

Later that evening workers were huddled into the construction trailer, used as an office. They were drinking and laughing.

Dave stumbled across the room to set his drink down. Slurring his words he said, "I think I had too much booze. I need a joint." He sat on the desk, pulled out a bag and some papers and started rolling a joint.

Pete said in shock, "What are you doing?"

"I'm rolling a joint."

"I know that. But, here?"

"It's a party, ain't it?"

"Well… yeah."

Highway to Hell

At this point Dave was driving a Pontiac Firebird. Even though it's body looked pretty rough with grey primer here and there to cover the Bondo, it was very fast, 350 horse power to be exact. Going home after the party Dave drove his car at about 80 mph and wandered back and forth a bit on the road. He passed a cop car under the overpass. The cop turned on his lights and siren and sped out onto the road in pursuit. Dave sped up to get away. He didn't need any trouble. Slowing down enough to make the corner he swerved onto the road into the subdivision where his parents lived. As he raced around the corner he tossed a bag of dope in the bushes. Racing down the suburb streets he lost control, spinning out, and slid into the front yard of one of the houses. The cops pulled up in front of the house. One officer got out of the car and quickly flung open the door of Dave's car. He grabbed Dave by his arm and dragged him out of the car. Dave was so drunk he could barely stand up.

With a certain sense of pride the officer said, "We got you, now. You son of a bitch."

The other officer walked up to the two. Going from bad to worse, Dave's parents pulled up behind the cop car and got out of the car to watch with great disappointment.

The arresting officer said to the other officer, "Cuff this guy and pat him down."

Time to Get Right with God

Dave's parents were going out of town for Christmas and, when he called from jail, they told him that they weren't going to be able to help him this time. They had their plans and basically were tired of bailing him out all the time.

Once in the jail cell depression hung over Dave like a heavy dark cloud. He banged his fist on the bunk mattress. "God, I can't believe I'm still this stupid" He bowed his head in reverence to God. "All I got now is you, Father. My folks can't help me. I'm in a fix, again." He looked up as if he could see God as he prayed. "You get me out of this one I promise that I will check out the Bible stuff that Zoe's into… I got to do something. Thanks in the name of Jesus Christ."

The next morning, Christmas day, an officer led Dave into the front foyer. Rev. Holder, Jed's dad, was standing in front of the counter.

Surprised to see him there Dave said, "Rev. Holder. What are you doing here?" Rev. Holder replied,

"Jed told me he saw you being arrested last night. I knew your folks were leaving town this morning and I could not bear seeing you spend Christmas day in jail."

"Isn't there a bail?"

"They're releasing you into my custody. They do that sometimes for clergy."

"Thank you so much, sir. I am so sorry you have to go through this."

Home Bible Fellowship

Zoe picked Dave up and took him to his first Bible fellowship. He could tell that she was jazzed about him going. Once there, several people sat in chairs in a circle in Sandra and Steve's living room. Dave sat next to Zoe on the couch. Sandra and Steve were seated in two chairs at the head of the room. They sang songs about God and Jesus Christ and prayed. Dave was intrigued by how positive and uplifting their prayers were, a nice change from that cry-in-my-beer stuff. They thanked God like He had already given them their answer. That was just fascinating to him. But, what came next blew his mind, so to speak. Sandra talked about hearing from God by way of the manifestations. Then, she explained, looking directly at Dave at first, that it was by way of tongues, interpretation of tongues and prophesy that we would hear from God exactly what we needed to hear. Then, one by one, she called on three folks. The first one spoke in another language followed by English. It was in first person as if God was speaking directly to the group. In English it was beautiful, very encouraging and comforting words. The second person did like the first and the last person only gave a message in English. Dave just couldn't keep his eyes closed. He had to see this amazing sight.

After the formal part of the meeting Dave and Zoe snacked on cookies and drank coffee with Sandra by the dining table. Others talked in the living room nearby.

Sandra wanting some feedback from Dave said, "Well, what did you think?"

"Well, for one, I'd never heard speaking in tongues. Very interesting." Sandra explained, "Those who have the gift of holy spirit have the ability to speak in tongues. It comes with the gift."

"Cool."

Zoe said, "I liked the teaching. God is spirit and must be worshiped in spirit and in truth."

Steve walked up to join the conversation.

Dave complimented him. "Great teaching, Steve. We were just talking about it. I like the part where you said, 'God is spirit and He can only communicate by way of the spirit.' Then, you told us how to get born again of God's spirit. I never was really sure if I was even saved but now I know from the Bible that I am. I believed God raised Jesus from the dead since I was a young boy. I guess, I've been saved all along. Sure is good to know!"

Steve responded, "Yeah, it's simple. Once you get the gift of holy spirit you can have fellowship with God."

"Well, it seems logical... I used to think God could communicate with you by the third eye. I was wrong. Clearly you have to receive holy spirit to hear from God."

Steve responded, "God is spirit and he can only communicate directly to that spirit inside of you when you get born again."

"How long have you guys been here doing this?"

Sandra said, "We've only been here two months. We volunteered to go to an area where there were no fellowships. These people here are all folks we witnessed to since being here."

"Wow. That's impressive!"

"Well, we've got plenty more to teach. Next Sunday at 11 is another meeting."

"Sure, I'll check it out. Hey, I want to know more about speaking in tongues."

Seizing the opportunity Steve said, "What you doing tomorrow night?" "Nada."

"C'mon by after 7 and I'll show you more."

Power from on High

Dave sat at the dining table with Steve and Sandra. Each had a Bible on the table in front of them. Dave had his Gideon's Bible.

After some casual fellowship Steve began to teach Dave

some details about speaking in tongues. "OK. First, I want to emphasize what I taught last night. That once you confess Jesus as Lord believing God raised him from the dead your saved and you receive the gift of holy spirit. God given abilities come with the gift." Dave said, "OK. I got that."

"Let's go to Ephesians 1:3."

Steve and Sandra quickly found the place while Dave stumbled through looking in all the wrong places for the book. Sandra reached over to help Dave find the spot. As she thumbs through the pages she said, "Corinthians, Galatians, then Ephesians. Here it is."

"Thanks."

Steve said, "Sandra, would you read that for us?"

"OK. 'Blessed be the God and Father of our Lord Jesus Christ, who has blessed us with all spiritual blessings in heavenly places in Christ."

"See, God has blessed us with all spiritual blessings. When God says all He means all. He didn't say some. If I could speak in tongues and you couldn't then He couldn't say 'all'. But, it's like, if I put a million dollars in the bank in your name but you didn't know you had it, could you spend it?"

Dave shook his head. "No."

"The reason people who are born again don't speak in tongues is either they don't know they got it or they don't believe."

"OK."

"So, we have been blessed with all spiritual blessings. No one has more or less. Speaking in tongues is part of that 'all'. You already have the ability. It came with the gift of holy spirit."

Remembering back Dave said, "You know, I thought I spoke in tongues once... but it was too easy."

Sandra responded enthusiastically, "It is easy! In the book of Acts when the apostles first spoke in tongues it says they spoke in tongues as the spirit gave them utterance. They did the speaking but God gave the utterance."

"What do you mean?"

"It was their responsibility to speak but what they spoke was God's responsibility."

Steve continued, "The word speak in the Greek means to speak without reference to the words spoken. You just start speaking without thinking about what is being said."

"Then, what am I saying?"

"You don't know what you're saying but it is another language. I met a girl from Africa that knew French, English and her native tongue, Kikongo. She went to a meeting where most of the people there only knew Kikongo. One person got up to speak in tongues and interpret. The tongue was in French and the interpretation was Kikongo. The person speaking didn't know French but she did. She said the interpretation was the sum and substance of what the man just spoke in French."

"That's pretty amazing," Dave said. "The time, I thought I spoke in tongues, it sounded like French."

Sandra said, "It may have been... The Bible says, I can do all things through Christ. If you have all spiritual blessing and you can do all then it's up to you."

"It all makes good sense but I haven't lived a very clean life and I just don't see how I deserve that."

Sandra smiled tenderly. "No one deserves it. It's not of works but by God's grace."

"What's it for?"

"In a believers' meeting you can give a message from God to that particular group. In your private prayer life you can make intercession for the saints and sometimes in situations, when you're just not sure what to pray for, you can pray in tongues and pray for the exact need. Plus it builds up the spirit that God gave you." "Interesting."

Steve in his eagerness said, "So, you want try it?"

Dave chuckled and said, "Sure, what do I do?"

Sandra moved over to the chair beside Dave and held his hand. "It's just as easy as when you did it before and you thought it was French. So... now, just take a deep breath and relax. Close your eyes."

Dave closed his eyes and took a deep breath.

Sandra continued, "It's easy. You're in total control. You by your freedom of will move your lips, your throat, and your tongue. Just start speaking without any consideration of what is being said. You can start and stop it by your freedom of will. Like this..." She simply spoke in tongues a bit.

Dave opened his eyes a moment to see then closed them. Sandra said, "I'll pray... Father, thank you for your wonderful gift of holy spirit and thank for giving us the ability to speak in tongues and magnify you. Thank you for Dave who loves you and wants to do your will. In the name of Jesus Christ... Now, speak in tongues."

Dave opened his mouth and spoke in tongues briefly then stopped.

Sandra said excitedly, "That's it! If you can speak in

tongues a few words then you can speak in tongues much. OK. Do it some more."

Dave spoke in tongues a little more boldly for a sentence or two. His eyes popped open. "I did it. I can't believe it. I did it!"

They hugged each other. Dave had tears of joy rolling down his face.

Dave went home that night speaking in tongues all the way home. He really still didn't know a lot about it but he knew, from the Bible, that it was God's will. He truly felt blessed by God and knew deep within that he was on the right track. It was like when he got an immediate answer from God when in jail. From the moment he heard speaking in tongues he just knew, that he knew, that this fellowship was exactly where God wanted him.

The next day Jed and Dave sat on the porch in lawn chairs at Dave's folk's house. On the side table an ashtray was full of ashes. They went through their ritual dope smoking routine.

Jed queried, "Where you been the past couple of nights?"

"Zoe turned me onto a great Bible fellowship Thursday. And, last night I went over to learn some more."

"What makes this different from our last experience?"

"When they spoke in tongues I knew that I was where God wanted me to be. Don't know any better way to explain it but in the depths of my soul I just knew!!!"

"Maybe I'll check it out. Not so sure about the tongues. But, after all, I survived the Rectification Church."

They both laughed.

Chapter 9

God Sent His Word and Healed Them

As the months passed by Dave continued to read and write, only this time his reading was books on Biblical topics and his writing was to glorify God like he had promised God when he started writing. He enjoyed playing Bob Dylan songs at one time but it had been a while since he played. He dusted off his lonely acoustic guitar and started reworking one of Dylan's songs. He took the song "Don't Think Twice, It's Alright" and rewrote the lyrics. It went like this:

Don't Think Twice, Thank God in Christ

Ain't no use in worry doubt and fear, babe
There ain't no troubles, anyhow
Ain't no use in worry doubt and fear, babe
When you got the Word of God

You can live a life and give it more abundantly
That's power in your soul for you to see
What God has promised you can surely be
Well, don't think twice, thank God in Christ

Ain't no use in living life without, babe
When you've got the grace of God
Ain't no use in living life without, babe
You're out of debt 'cause you've been bought

Well, you used to be thinking about your daily needs
But now you live in peace and you've been freed
Now you're seated with God's son in the heavenlies
Well, don't think twice, thank God in Christ

Ain't no use in starting out your day, babe
Without lookin' to the Lord
Ain't no use in starting out your day, babe
Without the Word of God, your sword

When the rooster crows at the break of day
Look out your window for some time to pray
God will hear the petitions that you make
Don't think twice, thank God in Christ

When he had the song mastered he played it for the Bible fellowship. He had the Dylan nasal twang down to a tee. Everyone really enjoyed his rendition of the classic song.

At this point Dave was fully engaged in fellowship and Jed enjoyed hearing about it but only would go every now and then. Dave had taken a Bible class and was really wanting Jed to take it. However, Jed still felt he was betraying his dad by doing something from a different ministry. Jed had been having trouble finding a job. He wanted one that was within walking distance since his car recently died. So, Dave told him to believe God to meet his need. A couple of days later Dave found a handwritten note on his folks' door. It was in an envelope with a logo from the church that Jed's dad pastored. It read:

Dear Dave,

God bless you!

You weren't home and I wanted you to know right away. I got a job 2 miles away! God did supply my need just like you said. Plus, today I got a refund check from an airline mix-up. I mean, when two important events like that happen within two hours of each other, it's got to be the manifestation of what the abundant life from God really is! It's exhilarating! I told my dad and he was very excited for me. So, yes! I want to take that class.

I guess, I'll catch you on the flip-flop.

Jed

As the months went by Dave, Jed and Zoe continued in the things of God. Dave and Jed got a place of their own and were doing quite well. Dave and Jed took a couple more Biblical research classes; Zoe was busy with college work and missed those. Dave and Jed were able to get around the Bible very well at this point. Understanding how the Bible fits together and how to rightly divide the word of truth was an exciting adventure. They learned from II Peter 1:20 that no prophecy of the scripture was of any private interpretation. In other words no guessing on what it means. It is either plainly stated or the Bible must interpret itself which takes research.

They all decided to go to a state-wide ministry event in Fort Worth, Texas. They arrived on Friday although Dave traveled seperately because he had to work a full day that day. He got there just in time to get his luggage in the room and change into his suit for the opening meeting. Missing the opening comments a band was playing as he walked in. The music appealed to many of the rock and rollers in the group although they played other styles including some country rock. After the meeting a large group of people milled around the lobby talking and partaking of the refreshments available. They all looked very formal in their suits and dresses. Dressing up was the norm for the opening session. Some stood in line at a table getting registered. Dave, Jed, and Zoe stood together with name tags on talking about what they learned in the teaching.

Jed, looking down at his suit, said, "Not used to wearing a suit except for a wedding or a funeral."

Zoe responded, "I like the way you guys look. Sharp looking dudes! Mmmm, baby." Zoe grabs Dave by the arm and snuggles up closely to him.

Dave puts his arm around her waist. "So, this is all the Bible fellowships in the state."

Jed said, "Yea. Gives me a bigger picture of what's going on."

"You guys want a cookie. I'll go get you one."

"Sure!", Dave and Jed said simultaneously. They looked at

each other and smiled as Zoe walked over to the table filled with beverages and cookies.

As Jed and Dave continued in their conversation about the teaching a gentleman walked over to Dave. "Hey, can I pray for you?"

Dave said a little surprised, "Well... sure."

The gentleman put his hand on Dave's shoulder and closed his eyes. Dave closed his eyes.

He bowed his head and said, "God, thank you for this man. And, thank you for his hand and for restoring it. In the name of Jesus Christ."

The gentleman patted Dave on the back. "I looked at your hand and it was green. I figured God was telling me to minister to you. God bless. Got to meet someone." The gentleman walked off.

Dave looked at Jed and shrugged his shoulders. "Don't know what that was about."

Jed said looking at his hand, "Well, he said something about your hand. Maybe the one that got put back together."

Dave grabbed his hand and felt it. "Wow. I can't believe it! The numbness has gone away."

"You're kiddin'."

Tears streamed down Dave's face. "Nope. I've got feeling in it again. I can't believe a miracle just happen right before my eyes and I was barely aware it was happening. God is so good!!!"

Zoe walked up to the two with cookies and handed each a cookie and a napkin. "Here ya go!"

Dave said, still flabbergasted about a notable miracle, "You won't believe what just happened."

"What?"

"A man just came over, ministered to my hand, and walked away. Half my hand used to be numb and now it has feeling again."

"Wow. That is amazing."

"Something else just came to my realization, tonight."

"What's that?" Jed said.

"I haven't been depressed in months. I realized it when I heard the verse in Psalms tonight where it said, God sent His word and healed them and delivered them from their destructions... I had thought, I would be plagued with depression the rest of my life. God's Word is healing me!"

Grinning broadly Jed said, "Plus, you speak in tongues. That's perfect prayer. It also builds up the spirit in the inner man. I've watched you change. You're excited about living, now."

"Well, I've got something to be excited about." Dave looked over at Zoe and put his arm around her waist. "Hey, Jed, could we have a moment?"

"No, problem." Jed walked away.

Dave said, "Zoe, you saved my life by introducing me to the Bible. I actually understand now. I want to thank you from the bottom of my heart." "Yeah, it's been a great experience."

Dave grabbed both of her hands facing her more directly and looked in her eyes. She returned the gaze.

Dave looked down a moment then back to her eyes. "Zoe... Will you marry me?"

"Yes!!!" She practically jumped into Dave's arms hugging him. "I would be honored to."

Tears of joy streamed down both of their faces.

After the event Jed rode back home with Dave. They stopped at Steve's to hang out a bit before going home. There had been a hurricane hit the island while they were away. Steve had informed them that the power was out in their part of town. Dave's immediate response was, "I claim in the name of Jesus Christ that our power will be on when we get back." Dave had learned from the Bible that the name of Jesus Christ was a name above every name and when used was powerful. Well, when they got back home their power was on! However, no one else in that part of town had any power.

Open Door to Serve

A few weeks later Steve and Dave were sitting at a booth at the Waffle House. Their waitress, Sally, set cups of coffee in front of them, nodded and walked away. Steve prepared his cup with cream and sugar and Dave took a sip just as it was.

Dave said shaking his head, "I can't believe what's been happening. I get engaged and then with a simple call she bluntly calls it off and immediately hangs up. She's not returning my calls either."

Steve said, "Well, Zoe hasn't answered my calls either. Look, I'll go by and visit her. In the mean time we can pray and believe for her."

"I'm just surprised."

"Well, she's still young in the Word. She hasn't gone after it like you and Jed. I mean, you guys are into the Word every day. That's why you've grown so much."

"Yep, first thing in the morning we're up and speaking in tongues, making intercession for the saints." Dave took another sip. "You know, that's another thing... If this thing with Zoe would have happened a year ago I would have lost it. I don't get depressed like I used to. I'm concerned and saddened but I'm not depressed."

"It's amazing how much you've grown." Steve stirred his coffee and took a sip. "So, how you guys liking your place."

"The place is great. Just what we prayed for. And, we got a great living room that would be great for fellowship if you wanted to have one there."

"That's what I wanted to talk to you about. Our fellowship is getting too big and we need to branch out. Sandra and I were talking and we would like to start doing a Bible study at your house. Sandra or I could come over from time to time as a support. You and Jed have done a great job of teaching in fellowship and we're confident you could handle one on your own with our support."

"Wow. That's awesome. Are you sure?"

"Philippians 4:13 says, 'I can do all things through Christ which strengthens me'. God made you able. All you need to do is have prayer and a short ten minute teaching. You both know how to speak in tongues and interpret and prophecy so when one of us are over we can do that also. That's all you need!"

Dave said, "What should I teach?"

"Just use some of the ministry publications. Makes it easy. Teach the same thing; you can't go wrong." Steve pulled out a pocket Bible and flipped through some pages.

Sally, the waitress, walked up to the table with their food.

Steve continued, "Look at this in II Corinthians 9:8...'And God is able to make all grace abound toward you; that ye, always having all sufficiency in all things, may abound to every good work.' See God is your sufficiency in all things and He will be there for you every step of the way!"

After setting the plates on the table the waitress, Sally, said, "Wish I knew God would be there for me every step of the way."

Dave, excited to be able to share God's Word, spoke up, "Well, He can. You just have to know and believe God's Word."

Sally shaking her head a bit said, "This is amazing. I just prayed to God this morning for some answers and here you are sitting at my station with a Bible. I'm fixin' to go on break after I ring up a customer. Do you mind if I join you."

Steve patted his hand on the seat of the booth. "Sure, we'd love to have ya." Sally walked over to the cash register and rang up a customer. She gathered the customer's change and pulled off her apron. Then, she went to the booth to join them. Dave scooted over to make room for her.

Sitting down she said, "I'm Sally."

"I'm Steve."

"I'm Dave... Yep, the Bible has answers. How can we help ya?"

"Well, I'm living with my grandmother. I have two kids and because of circumstances, that I don't want to go into, my children are in custody of the department of human services. I've got to get a place of my own to be able to get them back. I haven't been able to make enough to get a deposit, much less the rent."

Dave said, "God wants you to get your need met." Dave grabbed Steve's Bible and flipped through the pages. "Here, it is. Philippians 4:19, 'But, my God shall supply all your need according to his riches in glory by Christ Jesus.' When God says all He means all. God's Word promises He will supply all your need. You have to believe that and confess it."

"Sounds too easy."

Steve added, "God is big enough. We just have to believe that He will do what He promised."

"I don't know if I'm there yet."

Dave looked her straight in the eye and said, "Look. I guarantee, that if you start coming to our Bible fellowships regularly, that in a month you will have your own place and your kids back. I claim that in the name of Jesus Christ!"

Sally looked a little surprised at Dave's boldness. She looked down a second to take in what he said. Looking up she said, "OK. I'm putting you to the test."

Steve said, "It's God's Word you will be putting to the test and God backs up His Word."

She grabbed her ticket book and a pen. She tore off some paper from the back of the pad and started writing. "OK. I'll give you my grandma's phone number. You can call me tonight. I hope your right. I'm excited. But, only because you're excited." She handed the piece of paper to Dave and smiled. "Don't forget." "Oh, I won't"

Encounter with Zoe

Dave sat on the couch in the sitting room at Zoe's parent's

house. After a short wait Zoe came in. Dave stood up and reached out for a hug but Zoe quickly sat in the chair opposite the couch. Dave sunk back into the couch.

Zoe spoke up flatly not able to look Dave in the eye. "Hey, Dave, how's it going?"

"It's good."

"How did court go for that DWI?"

"Well, I pled guilty but I had the opportunity to speak. I told the judge about my recent involvement in the Bible fellowship and that my life was turning around. The judge was kind and lenient and gave me one year probation. With my record he could have easily tossed me in jail. God is soooo good."

"That's great, Dave. I'm glad for you."

Dave looked down at the floor then said, "Hey, Zoe, you haven't been answering my calls and it's been a while since you've been to fellowship. Is everything all right?... You just went totally cold after I asked you to marry me... I understand. There's no rush."

"Look, Dave, I just need some time to myself. It's not something you did." "Well, let's talk about it."

"Look! I don't want to talk about it. I just have to sort some things out on my own. So, I would just like you to quietly leave and give me some space. OK?" Looking bewildered Dave said, "But...".

"No! Give me some space..." Zoe slapped her hands on the arms of the chair and yelled, "Please!"

"OK!" Dave said with frustration.

Right Place at the Right Time

Dave and Jed had been running their Bible study in their home for a couple of months. Sally had been very faithful to come to their meetings but they weren't getting much response to their witnessing. Oh, they had a couple of people come out of curiosity but they really weren't serious enough about it and didn't stick around.

One night Dave and Jed decided they were going to be strong in the Lord, get off their ass, and get out and talk to people on the street. Dave prayed, "Heavenly Father, thank you for our efforts to find someone who will really want and need Your Word. Thank you that You work in us mightily to be at the right place at the right time with the right words for someone to get exactly what they need. In the name of Jesus Christ, amen." Dave looked up at Jed, "So, where do we go?"

Jed looking inspired said, "God Knows! In the name of Jesus Christ, God, show us where we need to be."

Dave said,"The seawall."

"I was thinking the same thing."

Once there, Dave and Jed waited for a gap in the traffic and then ran across Seawall Boulevard to the sidewalk on the seawall. They stopped and turned to each other.

Dave said, "OK. Let's pray." Jed moved a little closer to Dave so that he can hear better. They kept their eyes open looking at each other like they were having conversation. Dave continued, "God, thanks for pointing out clearly where we need be for someone who desperately need Your Word.

Thank you that we can make a difference in someone's life. In the name of Jesus Christ."

"Amen."

Dave looked to the left and then to the right. "Which way you want to go?" "That way." Jed pointed to the left.

"That's exactly what I was thinking."

They walked down the Seawall Boulevard sidewalk. Dave made conversation as they walked. "Well, I talked to Steve and Sally's going to start going to their fellowship. It works better for her work schedule."

"Well, she'll be well taken care of there."

"Yes, she's excited. She just wants to be around believers as much as possible... I'm still amazed that she has her own place and her kids back. God really pulled that one off for her."

"Yeah, that's really cool."

"Yeah, she doubled and tripled her usual tip intake. She could have almost paid her rent just in the coins she collected... Just wish Zoe would come back." "It's free will, man."

They approached a man sitting on the concrete bench looking out to the gulf. Dave said, "Hey, let's talk to this guy."

They made their way toward the man and Jed said, "Hey, how's it going? Nice night."

Adam shifted around on the bench to better face them and said flatly, "Yea, it's alright."

Jed continued, "I'm Jed and this is Dave."

"I'm Adam".

Dave added, "Glad to meet ya." Jed wasted no time. "The reason we're out tonight is that we've started a Bible study in our home and we're out seeing who might be interested. Have you got any questions about the Bible?"

Adam furled up his face questioning. "Have I got questions? It's one huge question mark."

"Well, Jesus Christ said in John 10:10, 'I am come that they might have life and that they might have it more abundantly.' It would be enough to have abundance but Jesus Christ said more abundantly. That's what's available. Either he lied or he told the truth. I believe he told the truth."

Adam nodded, "Of course, he told the truth."

Jed flipped through his Bible to find a verse.

Dave added, "In the same verse Jesus said that the thief comes not but for to kill, and to steal, and to destroy. That sets in contrast to the more abundant life." Jed pointed to his open Bible. "There's more. In Psalm 103 starting in verse 2." Jed sat down on the bench next to Adam so that he can read along with him. He pointed at the verse where he started reading. "Bless the Lord, O my soul, and forget not all his benefits." He looked at Adam. "There's benefits. The more than abundant life is a benefit. Then, it reads 'Who forgiveth all thine iniquities; Who healeth all thy diseases;'...When God says all He means all with a capital A double L. All. God said it and He meant it. 'Who redeemeth thy life from destruction;' No matter how messed up a person's life can get God can redeem them from that destruction."

Adam shaking his head in disbelief said, "You know I just prayed to God that I needed an answer and I needed it now. Then, you two walk up telling me about an abundant life."

Dave added, "More than abundant."

Adam chuckled, " OK. More than abundant. If you can

show me how to live more than abundant then I'm interested."

Jed said patting him on the shoulder, "We can and will."

Mobile Fellowships

In the months ahead Dave, Adam, and Jed pretty much made up the Galveston fellowship. Dave's friend, Jake, saw the positive changes in Dave's life and checked it out a few times. Jake enjoyed the fellowship but thought fellowship in the home was weird. However, he still smoked pot on days that they weren't having fellowship. He wanted to keep a clear head when the Word was taught so he refrained from his habit on those days. But, after fellowship he would go home and smoke a joint before going to bed. Dave and Jed didn't really see the harm in smoking dope but they stopped smoking for the most part because they didn't want the ministry to get blamed. Dave would be enticed occasionally to have a puff with an old friend. But, that was rare because he spent the vast majority of his time with the household believers in the area.

The guys shared with others what they were learning but were having a hard time getting people to come to fellowship. Then, Dave had the brilliant idea to bring the Word to them. So he announced at fellowship that they would go out somewhere public for the next fellowship. He asked them to keep their eyes peeled for a good location where people could overhear them.

When the time came, Dave was at the head of the room in front of a coffee table. "Well, God bless. As promised tonight we are going to go out to have our fellowship. Instead of trying to get people to come to us, we're going to bring the Word to them... Jed, would you pray."

Jed bowed his head and said, "Father, God, thank you for Your Word, how it has enlightened the eyes of our understanding. Thank you for great doors of utterance as we speak Your Word to hungry hearts and thank you for miracles, signs, and wonders following. In the name of Jesus Christ."

"OK. Adam, I like your idea of going to a hospital lobby for our fellowship. Did you check out a location?"

"I did. The university hospital medical towers will work great. There's two towers and there's a lobby immediately off the elevator entrance on each floor." "That's perfect. We can walk there since it's so close... Let's do this!"

Dave grabbed a pocket Bible off the table and handed it to Jed. He picked up the other one for himself.

Dave, Jed and Adam walked over to the two medical towers at the university hospital. They stopped directly in front of the two towers checking it out.

"Looks like Med Tower One isn't very active. There's lots of activity in the second tower." Adam said.

Dave nodded his head. "Well, we want people in ear shot of the teaching so tower two it is."

Once in the building they made their way to the elevator and stopped and looked at each other.

Dave asked, "Jed, which floor should we go to?"

"I don't know. Try seven."

Elevator doors opened and they walked in, headed for the seventh floor. They popped out of the elevator into the lobby. Several comfortable chairs and end tables were placed in the room for family and visitor fellowship. A lady in her mid-forties, Alice, sat in the room reading a magazine. The guys sat down on the couch and arm chair facing her. Dave was a little uncertain on how to open up a meeting in this new environment.

Finally Jed broke the ice. "Hey, Dave, what was that you were going to show me in the Bible."

"Oh, yeah. Thanks for reminding me. You'll like this!" He pulled out his pocket Bible. Then, Jed pulled out his. Dennis leaned in a little closer to hear. The lady looked up over the magazine she was reading and looked back down.

"I've been studying about the goodness of God. God is light and in Him is no darkness at all. No darkness means no, I said NO, darkness at all. Not one iota. Go to I John chapter 1 verse 5." Dave went on to teach for a few minutes then concluded, "So, there it is. God cannot be tempted and He tempts no man with evil. So, He's not testing you. God is good always. The adversary, or the devil, is blaming God for evil but God is light and in him is no darkness at all. Pretty neat stuff, huh."

Adam responded. "Yeah. I love that. God is light. Great stuff!!!"

They paused for a moment. Alice had put her magazine down and was intent on what Dave was saying during his teaching. "I couldn't help but overhear you, boys. I was wondering if you could take some time and pray for my daughter." Dave enthusiastically responded, "Sure. Be glad to."

Alice got up from her chair. "Thank you so very much. Follow me. She's not far." She started moving toward the hospital room then stopped and turned to the guys. "Oh, by the way, my name is Alice." Dave, Jed and Adam introduced themselves in return.

They followed Alice into a private room. A boy, Jimmy, about 10 years old was sitting in a chair by his sister. His older sister, Beverly, was sitting up in her bed.

Putting her hand on Beverly's shoulder Alice said, "I just met these young men studying the Bible. I asked them if they would pray for you. This is Jed, Dave and Adam. This is my daughter, Beverly."

Beverly said, "Thank you very much for coming."

Jimmy squirmed around in his chair looking very uncomfortable. He stood up and put his hand on his mom's arm. "Mom, who are these men. I don't..."

Alice interrupts, "It's fine, Jimmy. They want to help."

Jimmy slumped back down in the chair.

Dave approached from the other side of the bed and addressed Beverly. "Do you believe that God can heal you?"

"I do. I've been praying for a miracle. The doctors are so negative."

Dave was unsure about the young boy being in the room thinking about how Jesus Christ made the unbelievers get out of the room when ministering to a dead damsel. But, after asking God silently he felt that it was alright for the boy to remain. Dave put his hand on her shoulder. Jed and Dennis closed their eyes while Alice bowed her head. Jimmy observed intently.

He prayed, "Father, God, You created the heavens and the earth and all things are possible to him that believes. Thank you for your mercy and grace for Beverly and for manifesting your healing power. Thank you for eliminating the cancer in her body and completely and absolutely restoring her health. In the name which is above all names, Jesus Christ."

Jimmy's eyes were wide open when Dave opened his eyes.

Jimmy said in amazement, "How did you know she had cancer?"

"I didn't know. But, God knew."

Chapter 10

Bold Faced Attack

Zoe had asked her dad if she could use his office downtown to study. So he gave her the key to the place. She took her Bible and when she got there she went directly to the desk and sat down. Tears were rolling down her face. She sat the Bible on the desk and was flipping back and forth with some frustration. Meanwhile Dave arrived at Zoe's family's house.

Mr. Anderson answered and said, "Dave! Good to see you, son."

"Good to see you, sir. Is Zoe home?"

"No, she went to my office to work on some college work. I'll tell her you dropped by."

"I appreciate it."

Back at the office Zoe sat at the office desk with an open Bible off to the side. Her head lay on the desk as she sobbed. She raised up with tears running down her face and pleaded, "God, I just can't make sense of this anymore. I just can't seem to find a way out of this deep depression. It's been hanging over me like a cloud. I am sick of this mental anguish over and over again. I can't even stand to be around anyone anymore... I'm sorry, God, that I have to do this... forgive me but I don't see any other way out." She opened one of her dad's desk drawers, pulled out a pistol, put it to her head and sobbing uncontrollably pulled the trigger.

Subtle Attack

Dave was sitting on the porch steps with his arms folded on his knees and head cradled in his arms. He raised his head with tears still dripping down his cheeks. "This is shit, God. How can this happen? I knew, I had to go see her. I should of gone to the office. Damn it!!" He laid his head back on his arms. Shadow strolled up to where Dave was sitting. "Hey, man, how's it going? Heard the bad news."

Dave raised his head. "I'm ok."

Shadow sat down by Dave. "Man, that's a bummer... You don't look ok." There followed an uncomfortable dead silence.

Shadow continued, "Haven't seen ya in a while. Heard you got religious..." More silence ensued.

Shadow really had one thing in mind. "Well, you ain't quit smokin' have ya."

"I have a toke every now and then. Pretty rare though since we started doing a Bible study in our home. Jed and I agreed to cool it."

"Well, if there was ever a time to do it this is it. Looks like you could use some pain killin'. I've got some good stuff, if ya want."

"Sure, why not?"

Shadow pulled out a joint from his shirt pocket and lit it up with a big hit. They took a few hits in silence.

Breaking the silence Shadow said, "I really don't see what you get out of that Bible stuff."

"That's the best thing that's happened to me. All I know is, I used to be manic depressive a lot but now I'm not."

"You don't look better. Wasn't Zoe in this with ya.'"

"Yeah, she dropped out a few months ago."

"Well, can't see it got her anywhere. She's dead."

Dave laid a hard punch on Shadows check. Shadow flew off the porch onto the ground with his joint flying in the air. Dave instantly stood over him.

Shadow rubbing his check said, "What the..."

"You son of a bitch!" Dave was shaking with anger.

"OK. I was out of line." Shadow stood up brushing himself off and grabbed the smoldering joint.

"Just leave, please."

"Here, let me leave you a couple of joints... Peace, man."

"I don't want your fucking dope... Just leave, please!"

"OK, man."

Shadow walked away. Dave kicked the step on the porch and yelled out in pain.

All Things That Pertain to Life and Godliness

Dave and Steve sat on a bench by the sea on Seawall Boulevard. Steve met him there to minister to his heart.

Steve said, "Just wanted to follow up with you and make sure you're ok."

"I think I'm slipping a bit."

"How's that?"

"Well, an old friend dropped by yesterday offered me a joint and I took it like needed medicine. Jed and I used to smoke a lot. But, once we started doing a Bible study we agreed to lay off it. But, it's not because we thought it was bad but because we wanted to be a better witness. I've had a smoke every now and then since getting into God's Word. It helps me relax and I just reflect. But, I didn't like feeling like I had to have it yesterday."

"Why don't you think it's bad?"

"Well, I figure God put it on the earth. As long as it is in moderation it's fine."

"You want to know what the Word says?"

"Didn't know marijuana was in the Bible."

"All things that pertain to life and godliness are in it."

"OK. You've got my attention."

"In Galatians 5 the word witchcraft is pharmakia in the Greek. That's the word we get our word pharmacy from."

"What does it mean?"

"It means magical incantations by use of drugs."

"What does it say about it?"

"It says it's the works of the flesh and it's listed with a lot of other things we should avoid."

Dave responded "It says in Genesis that God gave man every green herb. Marijuana is an herb, right?"

"Yes, it is. But, it says he gave every herb for meat. If you ate marijuana it's high in nutrition but eating it raw won't get you high."

"Yeah, I heard that."

"It has to be heated up which causes a chemical change. That's why you have to smoke it. God's Word doesn't say He has given every green herb to smoke."

"Good point." Dave sat thinking on that a bit. "Oh... OK." He took a deep breath. "If it's in the Word... I quit. That's all you need to say. Been doing better without it lately anyway. I figure God knows better than I do and that's enough for me."

"That's what I love about you, Dave." Steve gave Dave a hearty slap on the back. "Once you see it in God's Word you change."

"I've got another question."

"What's that?"

"I was talking to Zoe's folks and they're torn up because they believe if a person commits suicide they can't be saved. They called it the unforgiveable sin." "Ok. That's in the Word, too." Steve pulled out a pocket Bible and started flipping through pages.

Chapter 11

Comfort During Tribulation

Mr. Anderson invited Dave over to talk over the details for the funeral. Mr. Anderson along with their son, Tim, and daughter, Sylvia, sat in the living room with Dave. Mrs. Anderson stood near the kitchen door.

Mr. Anderson said, "Well, Dave, you meant a lot to Zoe and we would like you to be one of the pallbearers."

"I'd be honored, sir." There was a long silence in the room. "I want you to know that I was pretty messed up until Zoe came along. She saved my life."

Mrs. Anderson replied, "That's very kind of you to say."

"I, also, want you to know that suicide is not the unforgiveable sin. I discovered scripture that says the contrary."

Mr. Anderson looked attentive. "OK. I'm listening."

"Romans 10:9 says that when you confess Jesus as Lord and believe God raised him from the dead then you're saved. When you get saved you get the gift of holy spirit. It's a gift and it's yours to keep. Zoe believed that verse and was saved."

Tim said scratching his head, "Can't you loose it when you sin?"

"Just a second and I'll find it." Dave pulled a pocket Bible out of his back pocket and found the verse. "In I Peter 1:23... It says...". He ran his finger down the verses and stopped. "'Being born again, not of corruptible seed, but of incorruptible, by the word of God, which liveth and abideth forever'. Corruptible seed is what you get when you are born the first time from your parents. Incorruptible seed is what you get from God when you are born again. It's corruptible seed because you eventually die. The gift from God is incorruptible. It cannot die. It's spirit."

Tim said still in doubt, "What about when you sin?"

"It's just like seed from your earthly father. If you break something or stop doing his will your relationship may not be very good but you are still his son or daughter. The same is true with God when a person gets saved. Your relationship may change but your standing as a son or daughter of God does not change." Sylvia added, "So, what about the unforgiveable sin?"

"Just as one can confess Jesus is Lord and get saved. If someone confesses the devil as Lord that is the unforgiveable sin... So, let me reiterate, Zoe is saved and we will see her when Jesus Christ returns."

Mr. Anderson said with a possible glimmer of comfort, "Son, I hope you're right."

Mrs. Anderson added appreciatively, "Thank you for telling that to us, Dave. That was very encouraging."

Light at the End of the Tunnel

Zoe's casket lay above the open grave while Zoe's family stood by the grave with Dave. Other family and friends including Jake gathered, some sobbing.

The preacher spoke from a portable podium at the head

of the casket. "And, finally to close, I want to read from the scriptures from I Thessalonians 4 starting in verse 13.... 'But I would not have you to be ignorant, brethren, concerning them which are asleep, that ye sorrow not even as others which have no hope. For if we believe that Jesus died and rose again, even so them also which sleep in Jesus will God bring with him. For this we say unto you by the word of the Lord, that we which are alive and remain unto the coming of the Lord shall not precede them which are asleep. For the Lord himself shall descend from heaven with a shout, with the voice of the archangel, and with the trump of God: and the dead in Christ shall rise first: Then we which are alive and remain shall be caught up together with them in the clouds, to meet the Lord in the air; and so shall we ever be with the Lord. Wherefore comfort one another with these words.' Amen... Let's bow our heads in prayer. Heavenly Father, thank you for all Zoe's loved ones and family today. Thank you for comforting their hearts and giving rest to their souls. In Jesus' name, amen."

People stood for a moment and some started to leave. Tears rolled down Mr. Anderson's cheeks. He turned to Dave and his family and said, "God is so good. While the preacher was reading the scripture I saw us all standing together with Zoe at Jesus' return. Now, I know of a truth that Zoe is saved. God showed me!" Zoe's family hugged each other and then Mr. Anderson gave Dave a big hug. "You were right. Thank you."

They stood there for a moment and Jake walks up to Dave. "Hey, Dave, could I get a ride. My folks dropped me off here."

"No problem."

As they drove away Jake said, "I hate funerals. Sort of bums me out." "Yeah."

"Hey, you want to smoke a joint?"

"Naw, I'm done with that stuff."

"La..la..look, I've been meaning to ta..ta..tell ya. This fellowship stuff your into is sort of wa..weird. I don't want you to end up like Zoe."

"Look. I'm better off with God's Word."

"I'm just warning you. This thing could be some kind of a ca..ca..cult." "Yeah, right!", Dave said sarcastically.

"I'm just saying. You were better off smoking dope. At least then, people weren't da..da..dieing around ya."

Irritated Dave said, "Now, that's enough!!!"

A police car from behind turned on its lights and siren. Jake pulled out a joint and started putting it down his pants.

Dave does a double take, "Damn, Jake, I better not get busted because of you." Dave pulled his car over. "Father, in the name of Jesus Christ I claim Your hedge of protection and we don't get busted."

Jimbo got out of the police car and walked over to Dave's car. Officer Ward was still busy talking to dispatch.

Dave rolled down the window. "What's the problem, sir?"

With some pleasure in his voice Jimbo said, "Dave Brinkley. We meet again. The reason I'm pulling you over is that you have a tail light out. But, seeing who we have here..." Then his voice became stern. "I think you both better get out of the car."

Dave and Jake looked at each other and got out of the car.

Jimbo said, "Hands on the hood and spread your legs."

As they put their hands on the hood of the car Officer Ward walked up. "What are you doing Jimbo?"

"What do you think I'm doing? Searching these two clowns."

"Well, normally I would search 'em. Stand up boys."

Dave and Jake turned to face Officer Ward.

Looking at Dave Officer Ward said, "Dave, since you really helped my niece out I'm going to cut you a break. Don't make me regret this."

Dave and Jake gave a sigh of relief as Dave said, "Who's your niece?" "Sally. You helped her get into her own place and her kids back."

"OK. Didn't know she was your niece."

"Well, I'm just going to give you a warning. You best stick with that Bible stuff. One step out of line and you're goin' down. And, by the way, your hair looks better in a pony tail but... you still look like a freakin' girl... And, get that light fixed."

Dave smiled broadly. "Thank you, sir."

Chapter 12

A Higher Calling

Dave, Jed and Adam walked up to the elevator door in the same medical tower that they did mobile fellowships before. At this point they had been to several floors sharing God's Word with folks. Whilst many got blessed with the Word they still had not gotten anyone new to fellowship in their home.

Dave turned to the guys. "OK. Which floor this time."

Jed said, "I was thinking 6."

Adam chimed in "Yes!"

Dave said hitting the up button, "Then, 6 it is."

When they got to the sixth floor they noticed the lobby was a bit differently laid out than the one before. They sat in a couch by a corner coffee table and a chair by that. An older gentleman, George, sat slumped down in one of the chairs across from where they were sitting.

Jed commented, "This looks way different from the other lobbies."

Dave added, "I wonder why? All the others look exactly the same."

They knew the routine by now so Dave opened it up. "Hey, Adam. You said, you found something in the Bible you wanted to share. Could you share that?" "Sure, glad to. I have never told anyone this. You remember when you guys first talked to me that night by the sea."

Jed and Dave nodded.

"Well, I was at the end of my rope that night and I had decided that I was going to walk out into that ocean and end it all. Then, you guys came along and started teaching me God's Word. You saved my life." Adam pulled out his Bible. "I want to show you this in Psalm 107:20." He started flipping through his Bible. Dave pulled out his and Jed looked on. "I haven't had any thoughts of suicide or depression since that day. I wondered at how I could have gotten delivered so simply and effortlessly. Then, I came upon this verse... It reads, 'He [God] sent his word and healed them and delivered them from their destructions.' It was God's Word that healed me."

Adam proceeded to teach his short teaching that he had prepared for the occasion. In closing he said, "So, God's Word is that big and it can heal and deliver anyone who believes... Father, thank you for the Word tonight that we can continue to believe and walk out on it. Thank you for continuing to heal and deliver people as they learn and apply your Word. In the name of Jesus Christ." There was some silence after. They normally had tongues with interpretation and prophecy in their home fellowships but never felt it appropriate in a public setting. However, it was big on Dave's heart to do so on this occasion. So, Dave piped in, "I think we should hear from God by way of the manifestations of the gift of holy spirit."

Jed nodded. "Great."

"I'll start." Dave spoke in tongues and interpreted. "Adam, would you speak in tongues and interpret?" Adam, who only recently learned how to manifest the spirit, boldly spoke in tongues and interpreted. "Jed, would you have a word of prophecy, please?" Jed brought forth a word of prophecy, a message directly from God. "Father, thank you for those words of comfort, edification, and exhortation and that we can take them to heart. In the name of Jesus Christ. Amen." George, the man sitting across from them, jumped up out of his chair with tears rolling down his cheeks. "God is great!!! I have two whole kidneys. Glory be to God in the highest who has blessed us abundantly. Great is God and his mercy endures forever. He it is that created the heavens and the earth and magnified His Word above all His name. Glory to God; I've been healed!"

George ran over to Dave, Jake and Adam shaking their hands and hugging them. They spent more time sharing God's Word with George then, because it was getting late, excused themselves. Dave gave George his phone number and they left.

At the bottom of the elevator ride the doors opened and Dave, Jed, and Adam walked out. The guys looked around the dimly lit floor as if lost.

Dave said, "This isn't where we got on the elevator. We are on the first floor, right?"

Jed said scratching his head, "Yeah. It's the first floor."

Adam added, "How did we end up here?"

Dave moved down the dimly lit hallway to a corridor to the right and sees an exit sign. "Here's an exit this way." Dave waved them over. Shortly they came to an open lobby area that looked closed and headed out the door. Once out they looked around a little disoriented.

Adam said looking perplexed, "We definitely didn't enter here."

They walked a little further down the sidewalk going away from the hospital.

Dave turned around to look at the two towers of the hospital. Dave stopped in his tracks. "Wait a second. We entered the other tower. How did we end up in this tower? No wonder everything looked different."

Jed added, "Well, we started in the elevator in that tower. Then, the floor we ended up on looked totally different from all the other floors."

Dave lit up and exclaimed, "Wow. God must have transported us like He did Enoch. That's how bad God wanted that man to get delivered..." Dave paused in deep thought. "He must of done it on the way up in the elevator. He sure pulled it off seamlessly."

Jed said shaking his head, "I know what I'm seeing but I'm still having a hard time believing it. No one's gonna believe this."

Dave agreed, "Let's just keep it to ourselves."

Adam said, "Yeah, let's."

They walked away from the hospital. Adam turned around walking backwards for a while, scratched his head as he looked back at the towers and turned back to walk with the others.

New Beginning

Dave, Steve and Sandra sat in the booth at the diner. Steve and Sandra ate their breakfast while Dave was finishing up.

Dave said, "I just want you to know, it's discouraging to be moving the Word and still not have many people come to fellowship."

Steve calmly replied, "Look. We're not responsible for people's responses. We're responsible for movin' God's Word... What about the girl from the hospital? She got healed from cancer. She was very thankful even though she never went to fellowship."

Sandra chipped in, "Thank God, she got delivered. She will always glorify God for that. When God gets the glory we've done our job."

Sally walked up with a cup of coffee to sit down at the table. "Ahh.... It's good to have a break."

Steve scooted over a bit for her to sit. "Glad you could join us."

Sally said in a bubbly fashion, "So what's up?" Dave said mundanely, "I was just complaining."

"What?, Sally said surprised.

"I've been getting discouraged that people aren't coming to our Bible fellowship. Wondering where I'm blowing it."

Sally responded emphatically, "You're not blowing it."

"Well, I missed it with Zoe. When I went to her house that day and she wasn't home I kept thinking I should go to her dad's office. I just wasn't listening to God."

Steve said, "As you learn more from God's Word you will be more confident and clear when you receive revelation."

"Yeah. You didn't miss it with me. You told me what to do to get my kids back. I believed and it came to pass."

Sandra said considering the incident, "Yeah, that was word of knowledge and word of wisdom."

Steve added, "And, when the girl was healed from cancer that was word of knowledge, word of wisdom, faith, and miracles. Look, we'll be teaching more on this soon."

Glancing at her Bible Sandra said, "Philippians 3:13 & 14 says to forget those things which are behind and reach forth unto those things which are before. We are to press toward the mark of the high calling of God in Christ Jesus." Agreeing Steve said, "That's right. We are called to a higher calling. We continue to set our affections on things above and move forward on God's Word." At that moment George, the man who got two whole kidneys, walked into the diner and looked around for someone to seat him. He glanced over and recognized Dave sitting in the booth and walked briskly in his direction.

"Dave!", George exclaimed.

George walked briskly to their table. Dave stood up to greet him and George gave him a great big hug.

"George, it's good to see you."

"I was released this morning. Tests have shown that my kidneys are completely healed."

"That's fantastic. Grab a chair and join us."

George grabbed a chair and sat at the end of the booth. "I lost your number. This morning I prayed that somehow I would run into you. So, I decided I needed a good breakfast and here you are. God is so very good. It's amazing."

"Wow. That's cool. I was wondering what happened to you."

"Well, I want to know more. Whatever church you are a part of I want to be a part of it, too."

"That's great. I will be having fellowship in my home tomorrow night. You are welcome to attend."

"Love to."

Sally said, "Oh, yeah. My schedule has changed and I am free for your fellowship, too, if you will have me."

"I'd love to. This is exciting!!!"

Sally added, "Yeah. We can move the Word together."

Dave said, "Hey. I want to pray."

Steve said in support, "Go for it."

"Thank you God that you have called us to a higher calling and that we are able to accomplish what you have called us to do because you made us able when you gave us the gift of holy spirit. Thank you for continued movement of God's Word that we as a team can see the greatness of your Word grow in our city. In the name of Jesus Christ."

THE BEGINNING!

About The Author

David C. Weekley

In my 20's I had been going to school off and on for 8 years and only had an Associate's degree to show for it. I was manic depressive or bipolar. I was depressed a lot. It would just hit me out of the blue and last for a week or so. In the field of psychology the best that could be done was take drugs. So I did. And, not necessarily on Doctor's approval. But, I was desperate. Drugs at best suppressed this dilemma but it was still there. Always came back up. And, it seemed that everything I tried to do just seemed to come out wrong. The scars were so deep that I figured I was going to be like that the rest of my life.

I knew the Bible had to have answers for me so I decided to try reading the new testament. I figured "new" had to be more pertinent than the "old" testament. At the end of the book of Revelation it warned against anyone adding to or taking away from those words. I knew I was guilty of that. So, I fell down to my knees and asked God to forgive me. I asked Him to send someone that could teach me how to understand this book without interjecting my own thoughts into it.

Not long after that, a friend of mine introduced me to group of people that were on a Bible outreach program. I had many questions and they answered them clearly and logically from the book itself. That, impressed me. I started attending their weekly fellowships and, was so excited about what I was learning that I started witnessing with them, or more accurately, observing them. I wanted to learn everything I could from them. I still had some issues going on but I knew I was on the right track. I took a Biblical research class and all of a sudden every question that I had about the Bible was being answered one by one. I found out that there is no condemnation to them which are in Christ Jesus. I found out I had sonship rights and one of those rights was righteousness. I was made righteous, not by my works but by the works of Jesus Christ. It was just as if I had never sinned. Oh, what a glorious realization. I realized God's great love for me and he made me righteous. In His eyes, I was righteous. Then, all the sin condemnation just melted away. I was freed from sin and the consequences from sin. I learned how to live one day at a time with fullness of joy.

As I absorbed God's Word I was completely and totally healed from Bipolar depressions. I quit drugs, too. Upon realizing that I wasn't getting depressed anymore I wondered... I would have thought it would have taken a great man of God to have laid hands on me and bam! I'm healed. But, this just crept up on me. Can't even pinpoint exactly when my deliverance happened. Then, that same week at a home Bible fellowship a man shared Psalm 107:20; He, God, sent his word and healed them and delivered them from their destructions. At that moment I knew that it was the greatness of God's word that healed me. And, I have never had a problem with depression since. As for school, I went back to college and finished my final 2 years in... amazing but true... 2 years. I thank God for those Ambassadors for Christ that showed me God's Word with precision and clarity. This was over 40 years ago. I'm just as excited about God's Word today as I was when I first started my Biblical quest.

www.ingramcontent.com/pod-product-compliance
Lightning Source LLC
Chambersburg PA
CBHW020326010526
44107CB00054B/1989